THE OTHER SIDE OF TRAVELLING

Travel stories without the filter

Daniel Greenwood

Copyright © 2019 by Daniel Greenwood

All rights reserved. No part of this publication may be reproduced, distributed, or transmitted in any form or by any means, including photocopying, recording, or other electronic or mechanical methods, without the prior written permission of the publisher, except in the case of brief quotations embodied in critical reviews and certain other non-commercial uses permitted by copyright law. For permission requests, write to the publisher, addressed "Attention: Permissions Coordinator," at the publisher below:

Daniel Greenwood Books

Ordering Information: Quantity sales. Special discounts are available on quantity purchases by corporations, associations, and others. For details, contact the publisher at www.dgreenwoodbooks.com.

First Edition

2 4 6 8 10 9 7 5 3 1

Thank you to everyone that gave me a helping hand throughout my travels. You restore my faith in humanity....well, most of you did anyway. Also, thank you to my family for putting up with me while I locked myself in a room and wrote this book. Finally, a big thanks to Kai, Valeska and Andy for their help with the editing.

INTRODUCTION

I remember the first time I decided that I wanted to travel. I was sitting in the lounge room of my grandparents, looking at the travel catalogues they had brought home. They were considering doing one of those packaged European tours. While skimming through the catalogues, I found one focusing on Greece. Obviously, it was just a catalogue. However, to my young five year old mind, the pictures of the locations were so interesting.

In particular, I have always had a real love of history and when I saw a picture of the Lion Gate, I knew I had to see the real deal one day (I later would, it was awesome). So, for the next ten years...well, to be honest I did nothing. I was a kid. I spent my pocket money on sweets and toys that would break after five minutes. I probably picked my nose. As I read more about history, I started to build a mental list of places I would one day visit. Egypt was always big on my list and it is still somewhere I hope to visit in the future.

At around fifteen years old, I got my first job at Target. For those of you who don't know, Target is one of those places that sells a little bit of everything. They tried to set themselves up in Australia as a more fashionable, upper class store. Well, I supposed compared to Walmart (or Primark for you European readers) it was. For me, it was simply cash.

I started my work as a cashier. However, in my eagerness to please my supervisor, when they asked me to take a position at the door greeting people, I mentioned that I was happy to do anything. I was just proud to be part of the team. The supervisor (who I swear was the devil incarnate) placed me on "the door" permanently. Officially, my job was to greet the customers as they came in and check bags and receipts on the way out. I got eight kangaroo monies (the official Australian currency) for this per hour.

There are a few points to note about this decision. I was fifteen years old. I was a hundred and sixty centimetres tall. I weighed fifty five odd kilos. I had so many pimples, you couldn't tell where blemishes ended and rest of my face began. My voice didn't break properly until half a year later. Picture me. The last line of defence against intruders and thieves. I would have been pushed over by a ninety year old woman trying to get to the discount doilies. I stayed there for four years.

My next job, while I was at uni, was working for a toll road company. The camera took the photo, I looked at the image and typed in the number plate. It paid really well and was a pretty easy job. I could eat and listen to what I wanted. I even listened to audio recordings of my lectures. This allowed me to work more while studying for my degree. The cash from this job was where I would get the bulk of my money to pay for the trips (at least the first big ones). Eventually, the work in the license plate typing section dried up, but I was "lucky" enough to move to the call centre. I did a horrible job. I was expected to finish a call in three minutes. I routinely took ten minutes. I just didn't see how it was possible to solve these problems in the way that they wanted me to. However, I did get to talk to two interesting customers.

One, was obviously a fan of the company. He was swearing at the automated machine before the line even dropped in to me. Calling it names and such, as if it would hurt the machines feelings. He kept swearing for a good minute after I received his call before he realised he was now actually talking to a real person. He took a deep breath and realised the error of his ways. As far as the gentleman was concerned, a real human required a different selection of profanity to that of the robot. Using combinations I wish I had written down, he swore at me for the next two minutes. I had to explain to him that he had the wrong number, and this was not the swear at people hotline. I was not sure why, but, he didn't seem to appreciate it. He swore with even more vigour. I hung up on him.

The other customer called and was all sweetness. He explained that he had travelled on the road a few times and had received a fine. He wanted to know if I could waive it. I had a maximum amount I could waiver, so I took a look to see if this was possible. When I pulled up his file, there was something like twenty thousand dollars in debt. He asked nicely if I could waiver it. I said no.

When I got off the phone, I did a quick calculation. When you travel on that road, they send you a letter asking to pay, plus a small admin fee. If you don't pay, they send you a reminder with an additional admin fee. If you don't pay that, they send it off to collectors who charge a hundred bucks. I assume they send a letter too. For each hundred dollars of debt, this guy would have received three letters. He had twenty thousand dollars in debt. So, he had to have received six hundred letters before he called us. Wouldn't you notice after the first hundred letters or so that maybe you should stop using the damn road? I lost my faith in humanity for a bit while I was working at that job. It was all the more reason that I had to get out in the world to get it back.

Throughout the next chapters, I will detail some of the funnier, crazier, stupider and most exciting adventures I had on the road. These stories I have in some way had the privilege of being involved. Perhaps you can be inspired or, more likely, learn from my stupid mistakes. Also, one quick side note. I assume this is obvious, but most of the names (and some of the appearances) of the people mentioned in this book have been changed for their own privacy. Just in case you were wondering.

AUSTRALIA

Did you read the sign?

While I was still in university to become a teacher, I went on teaching rounds in the Northern Territory. These are practicals, where you check out the profession and teach a few lessons, under the supervision of a qualified teacher to see if the world of education is for you. One year, there was an offer on the board. I could go and work in a nearby private school. Or I could go to a remote school in the middle of Australia, which was five hours from the nearest supermarket. I will give you two guesses as to which one I picked.

Australia still has a rich Aboriginal culture, but sadly, in many ways, it has been pushed up into the deserts. It seems that the land which was given back to the Aboriginals was easy to give as it had no real mining or commercial benefits. There is no land in the CBD of Melbourne or Sydney being given back to the original inhabitants.

To give you an idea of how big Australia is, it is a four-hour flight from Melbourne to Darwin. If I fly for four hours in Europe, I can pass over quite a few countries. I arrived, after the long flight, in Darwin, August of 2011. If you arrive any later in the year than this, the place starts to flood during the wet season. It is almost always thirty-two degrees Celsius but it is humid as hell. I got off the plane at midnight. I immediately started to sweat through my shirt.

Getting to the hostel, I had to share my room with three French girls. While I wasn't complaining about that, I was very uncomfortable with the sheer heat of four people in this small room. There was an air conditioner in the room, however, for one reason or another, the women did not want the thing on. It was three against one, and I lost that round. Peeling as many clothes off as I felt comfortable getting away with, around a bunch of strangers, I went to sleep. When I woke up, the three girls were naked and getting changed. They said "hi" and continued to get dressed. This encounter was my first taste of European behaviour. They are less concerned with nakedness than many people from Australia and the US. I didn't mind that the cooler wasn't on anymore.

The next day, I focused on getting food supplies as I had to wait a few days before the rest of the teachers arrived. We would all drive down together and get dropped off at the various schools along the way. I had put in a request for the most remote school I could get. While in Darwin I went and saw the crocodiles in the zoo, in their terrible enclosures. I felt sorry for them.

One day, I went to Mindil beach, where most evenings there are markets. I went there for the beach. I got my swimming gear on and went down to the water. The tide was low, so it was quite a distance to reach the water. When I looked out, there was no one swimming, which I thought was odd. I figured it was too hot for all of the others. Perhaps they didn't want to get burned in the sun. I was boiling, so in I went to cool off. I had a bit of fun, however, I didn't stay too long. As I walked back from the beach, all of them looked at me shell-shocked. Then one of them, with their mouth still gaping, pointed to a sign.

The sign had a lot of information on it, but basically said that you should not swim there because there are dangerous everythings in the water. Do not swim there. If you swim there, you will die. High chance of losing limbs. I should have noted the fact that the locals were not swimming as a tip to follow. However, I was just too stubborn. Travel tip No. 42: Do as the locals do and don't be an idiot and jump into crocodile-infested waters.

A quick side note. If you happen to visit the Mindil beach during the night market, keep an eye out for a guy named Geoff. He has a bunch of telescopes that you can check out cool stuff with. Always a lot of fun.

Men's business

Eventually after a few days, the other teachers arrived. I reluctantly moved from the hostel I was in, to another one across the street where my fellow colleagues were staying. The hostel smelled of mould.

We met an Aboriginal Elder named Steve. He was a super tall guy, with short curly hair. He had a huge smile and dazzling bright white teeth. Though, when I first met the man, he was quite shy and did not say more than a few words of greeting.

He was going to come with us and help educate the group on how things were up there, as well as, try to give us an understanding of how to deal with the Aboriginal kids. There is a stereotype that these children are not that bright. It is so very wrong. They are very smart. Some of the kids knowing up to five languages already. For comparison, at the time, I was struggling with one. However, they work on a completely different social system and that can clash with a western teaching style. To this day, I'm not that sure how effective the current teaching model is up there. Change is needed.

The first day, Steve took us out to a beach and to a nearby resort. It was here that he gathered the men in our group together and explained that he was going to take us on "special men's business". I was so excited to be getting access to this culture so early on, that I followed eagerly. He took us to a café and sent us in, in groups of two or three, to the toilet. Thinking that perhaps there was some traditional art that we were to examine, I followed.

We went into the toilet and towards the urinal, as instructed. It was there that we saw a one-way mirror. We could see all the guests eating as we pissed. It even looked a little like we were pissing into their food. Coming out of there, confused and unsure of how to take it, the elder was sitting there laughing his arse off. It was then that I got my first lesson, that while there is much to learn about Aboriginal culture, they can still make a joke. I had to shed the stereotypes I had in my head and go with the flow from then on. A couple of the stereotypes were well-meaning, but harmful, while others were down right stupid. However, either way, it was one of those moments that I think helped me to become a more aware person. Notice that I said the word "more". I still have way more to learn. Yet, it was a start. We were forbidden, by Steve, to say anything to the others and were told to send the next series of men in.

Later, when we were all done with the "men's business", we moved on. The girls were curious, but we said nothing. It did make for an intriguing conversation. Steve would continue to make jokes like this from time to time and I grew to appreciate his sense of humour. Especially, when I was in on the joke.

A cracker of a night

That night, we all went back to Mindil Beach Market. There were a number of neat people playing music and the night was going well. Some of the other student teachers were watching the sunset. At this point, I should be honest. They were friendly people, and I suppose in my own way, so was I. However, we had absolutely nothing in common. The result was a lot of awkwardness. It took me years to realise that I could just be me and that it was OK if people liked me or not. However, back then, I wanted everyone to like me.

So, in my head, I came up with a super smooth entrance to impress the other teachers. I went to join them and, thinking the sand would absorb my impact, dropped right on to my butt. The sand where they were sitting was already compacted from many years of tourists visiting to watch the sunset. As a result, when I landed on my coccus, I may as well have dropped a metre onto concrete. It hurt like hell. I like to think I kept a brave face and I don't know for sure what happened. Nonetheless, it hurt for weeks after. I had the feeling I at least fractured it. Not a smart move before a long drive into the desert.

The next day we started our drive down to Katherine where we would all be staying before we split into our various localities. To my luck, Steve would be coming down to my school to visit and show us around the local neighbourhood. The place I was going to work, Kalkarindji, was near one of the sites where the first really big protests to get the land rights back took place. It was the first successful attempt, and it set a precedent.

Along the way to Katherine, we stopped off at various sites including magnetic termite mounds and waterfalls. The whole way on the long bumpy drive in the desert my butt was killing me. Every pothole felt like a knife was being wedged right in. However, the seat was cushioned, so when I wasn't being assaulted with crippling pain, it was alright, I guess.

When we arrived at Katherine, the leader, a guy named Alan, explained that we would go to the gorge there (which is beautiful by the way) and canoe down a part of its lengths. He was doing a lot of work with the indigenous communities to help build an understanding between the two cultures. Even though he had done this many times before, as he explained to us the wonderful things we might see while there, his eyes lit up and you could feel the energy and enthusiasm radiating from his body. Along the walk down to the gorge, we got to see lots of wildlife. That made me a very happy boy.

Under normal circumstances, a canoe ride down a beautiful river sounds great, however, with the state of my rear end, I was not as excited as I had been the day before my injury. When I sat in the hard plastic seat of the canoe, I was even less enthusiastic. We set off though and started paddling our way down the river.

The view was spectacular. My team mate in the canoe was a girl by the name of Emily, that I had known since high school. By coincidence, we had both decided to be teachers and ended up in the middle of Australia on this crazy trip together. Emily and I had plenty of time to look at the gorge, because we could not get the canoe to go straight down the river. It can't have been more than two or three kilometres down the river. However, after all the zigging and zagging, we must have done ten kilometres of rowing. When we finally arrived at our destination, I was thankful for being able to get out of the canoe and just stand. We had lunch and a swim at the location where we stopped. It was at that moment that my next stupid idea took hold.

A number of the people in our group were jumping from a ledge into the gorge. For a short, hobbit like creature such as myself, it appeared to be very high up. One after another, they jumped. They asked me if I wanted to come. My head said no, yet, my ego said yes. So, with a big smile I climbed up. When I got there, my brain started having a very calm discussion with my ego. It went something like this:

"Ego, you are a fucking idiot. You are afraid of heights. You always say to people that 'God made you short as a sign you should stay close to the ground'. Now you are up on a ledge, and everyone is watching. You should go down and just chicken out man."

to which my ego replied:

"I can't chicken out. They will think I am a chicken."

My ego won the argument and I started to run towards the edge to jump off. It was then that I experienced an intriguing fact about the human body. I was moving forward fast. I wanted to build a lot of momentum before going over to make sure I cleared the cliffs and landed cleanly in the water. About half a metre before the edge, my autopilot kicked in. My ego told my legs to keep going, but my self-preservation put the breaks on. My legs stopped moving. However, with the momentum I had, I slid and nearly went over the edge anyway. If I had gone over after my freak out, I would not have had enough speed to clear the rocks at the base of the cliff.

Once again, Ego kicked in. It wanted to send me over that edge. With everyone watching, I overrode my instinct and jumped as far forward as I could. As I fell, I could see the water coming towards me. However, because of the aerodynamics and many other scientific explanations, I was rotating in the air. I was going to land right on my back. I managed to do the right manoeuvres in the air and almost got myself to the correct position before I crashed into the water. But, it was not enough. I landed with full force on my coccus. Pain spidered through my lower back. The water was not as soft for landing as I had hoped, and I almost couldn't swim properly due to the pain. However, my ego was happy because I didn't look like a chicken. All I did was take the risk of severely injuring myself, just to receive the reward of other peoples' approval. It didn't even work. Overall, a very stupid move.

Soon after, Emily and I got back into the canoe. She hadn't seen the jump and was a little confused why I was struggling even more to paddle. As I sat there in agony, I decided that I would do my best to stop Ego from making decisions again. It would not always work. However, I did sometimes manage to stop myself doing really dumb things. Sometimes.

Learning the hard way

Anyway, the next day, Kylie, Edith (two of the other student teachers) and I hopped into a car and drove the five hours needed to get to the remote town, known as Kalkarindji. Kylie was slightly older than the rest of us, had bushy blonde hair and seemed to have known Steve for a while. Edith was around twenty years old, with light brown hair. She was very enthusiastic to be there and seemed to have done a lot of research in the lead up to our visit. They would be my companions for the three weeks that I would be at the school.

As we made our way down, the girls and I saw a lot of nature, as well as, a lot of broken down cars. When something goes wrong with your vehicle out there in the desert, your options are rather limited. You can wait for a repair truck, but that could be hours. Alternatively, you can just ditch the car and get a lift. It would seem that option two was the more popular choice.

Luckily for us though, there were no issues with our car, so we arrived at Kalkarindji safely. When we finally got there, we got to see the effectiveness of the government's attempt to ban alcohol consumption in the area. There was a big pile of cans on the border of the town. It seems that those wishing to drink an alcoholic beverage, simply drive somewhere, buy their supply, drink it on the edge of the town and, when finished, walk home.

There must be better programs than that to stop the issues in many of these outback communities. I mean, just think about it for a second. If someone tells you not to do something, don't you want to do it? A lot of the population would riot if they were told they couldn't drink, but the Aboriginals have to suck it up? I am not a big fan of drugs, however, there shouldn't be separate rules on stuff like that based on the colour of your skin or what area of Australia you live in. Just my opinion.

On a positive note, the girls and I met some of the people that were actually a part of the original land rights protest. One guy was a man called Jimmy Wavehill. Wavehill is where a large portion of the Gurindji tribe camped to protest the land rights. So, really his name says all you need to know about his credentials. He was a charming man, with a broad smile, in a clean white shirt and a cowboy hat. I pictured Texas more than Outback from his appearance. He also seemed to be chuckling about everything. Happy guy.

I can't remember the exact numbers, but, in the course of the discussion he said to me something to the effect of, "I have ten children, fifty grandchildren and two great grandchildren." The population of the village was around six hundred. This means roughly ten percent of the whole village has this man's DNA coursing through their veins. Talk about being the heart and soul of a town.

The first night we were there, around midnight, I heard pattering on my roof. Wondering what it was and thinking it was some kind of animal running around, I got up. It was then that I saw a bunch of kids, their bright eyes glinting, full of energy, and gleaming white teeth from their smiles, which shone under the torch light. It seems that the 'cool' thing to do there when you're young is to run on rooftops at night. Their eyesight must be fantastic. If I tried that I would have broken my neck on the first go. Probably, before I even made it up onto the roof. Perhaps before I had gotten down the steps of the verandah.

Another evening, I experienced another example of the ineptitude of my body compared to these children when I played a game of football with the kids.

Australian Football is different from most other ball sports in the following way. You use your hands a lot and bounce the ball like a basketball. Another big difference is that the ball is shaped like an oval, so it doesn't bounce evenly. The rules of the game state that, you are permitted to kick it. If you want to pass it to a teammate using your hands, it must be done by punching it with a closed fist. I don't know where that rule came from. Maybe the people designing the game decided it was more "manly". A few years ago, they finally started a female league. It follows the same rules as for the men and the game is intense, quick and brutal at times. I guess it is easier to just check it out on YouTube. Type in "speckie" or "AFL mark" compilation into the search bar. Oh, and look up a professional game, they have to tackle each other for the ball and the goal umpire does a little dance every time a goal is kicked. I know it sounds, looks and is weird, but it is quite fun to play and watch.

I had to explain all that so that you understand that it truly is a game of skill. Skill, that I didn't have in broad daylight. The children were just wearing whatever they had on for school that day. We started while the sun was up and continued well into the evening. It was pitch black and the ball was bright neon yellow. But, I still couldn't see a single person on the field.

The kids, however, were having a full-on game around me, with scoring and everything. As far as I can remember, I am proud to say, I only got hit in the face five times. Luckily, there was no nose bleeds. Success is based on what goals you achieve. I set the bar low and limped across the line. I held my ground. But, I was very sore the next day.

A story and a show

One day, the Elder we had met in Darwin, Steve, took Edith, Kylie, Alan and I out to the river near the town of Kalkarindji. He made us pick up stones and told us to throw them in to the river. He explained that it was so that the nature knew we were there. I followed all his instructions. Any protection from getting eaten by hangry crocodiles is OK by me. I am not picky.

Throughout the next half an hour, Steve, in his slow, quiet voice, told us segments of the Dreamtime stories relevant to his people. He was not Gurindji. He instead came from a tribe called Warlpiri. The stories are different for each tribe and not all could be told without being initiated into the tribe. Nevertheless, the gist was a fascinating insight into one of the driving forces behind the culture.

At some point during the storytelling, he stopped, slowly looked around and said, "we have to leave." He told us there were bad spirits around. Again, I was with this man, in an area he knew very well and so I didn't want to argue. Getting up immediately, I walked with him back to the 4WD.

Kylie wanted to take one last photo of the river before we all left. We all turned around towards the car and then heard a scream. I turned around quickly and then started to laugh. Kylie had fallen in the water, and was sitting about one meter in from the edge, completely soaked with a wet camera. The elder just turned to her, shrugged, said "Bad Spirits" and walked off. I paid a lot more attention to him after that.

Around this time, I caught a super-infection. I hope I don't disappoint anyone by clarifying that I didn't get infected with superpowers. No flight. No super speed. I was bedridden with a temperature of forty degrees Celsius for two days and had so much snot coming out of my nose, I was seriously contemplating simply shoving a roll of toilet paper right up each nostril to make it stop. I was staying right near the school and I remember how I tried to drag myself across the courtyard to the school to start my lesson.

I was afraid that if I didn't do the lesson, I would not have enough hours of practical experience to pass my degree. Looking back at how stupid I was to put my life at risk for something like that, I just want to slap myself. I still do stupid stuff like that from time to time and really have to sit down and reevaluate things. Something like that is not worth such a risk. It isn't heroic, it's just dumb. Learn from me.

Luckily for me, the medical service up there is quite well supplied with all the good medicine. I was back on my feet soon enough, with a little help from antivirals and antibiotics. I made up the hours I missed without any problems.

Paul who?

We were told that the anniversary of the land rights movement was coming up. To celebrate, a few very famous, iconic Australian musicians were coming up to play a free gig for the community. I had heard the names of Paul Kelly, Dan Sultan, and Kev Carmody. However, I could not put a name to the faces or what type of music they were playing. I was told that each had built strong ties with the story of the locals there and everyone was excited about their upcoming arrival.

As the day approached for the concert and memorial march, the principal of the school explained that all the accommodation was booked and so, the bands would stay where we had been crashing (in the school library). We would be staying at the assistant principal's place.

I was cleaning up the dust in our humble abode before Kylie, Edith and I moved out. The dust inevitably penetrates every corner of the house given any chance. I was almost done, when three men walked in. I said a quick "Hello" and explained to them, "I will be just a few moments" as I was finishing off the cleaning for the coming guests. The three men were carrying a lot of stuff, so I figured they were roadies or the backup bands. I chatted with them briefly, then let them get comfortable and left the building. When I got outside, there was a whole crowd there waiting. I couldn't believe that they were all there for me, so I asked them what they were waiting for. They replied only in questions.

First, they asked me if I had spoken to the men. I said, "sure, they seemed nice." It was then that half the crowd explained to me that they were some of the famous musicians that would be playing that night. They said, I should give up my Australian citizenship for not knowing them before. After seeing them live, rocking the stage later that evening, I had to agree with their conclusion.

The musicians all took part in a memorial march to commemorate the forty-fifth anniversary of the movement. It was a very emotionally charged moment. Dan Sultan, Paul Kelly and Kev Carmody joined the march and talked to the people. Even now, thinking back on that day gives me goosebumps. Often, in the city, you are so far removed from such issues as the Aboriginal land rights movements that it seems like the whole process is over and everyone is happy. Being there, you could feel such energy from the participants. They are still protesting. Moreover, if what I felt on that day is any indication, they are not going to go down easily. The government might just have to listen to what they have to say.

On the road to nowhere

A few days later, after the area where the concert had been held was cleaned up, we moved back into the library. I was sitting outside my residence again and saw dust billowing into a cloud on the road. It came slowly closer. Finally, I could just make out what was going on. It was a girl. On a bicycle. In the desert. As she came closer, I could make out the features.

She was slender, with light brown hair tied back into a plait. She had a loose white shirt on, stained with dust and sweat, as well as riders leggings on. Her bike was surrounded by four bags hanging from various places on the front and back wheel. She must have had all her water and food in there.

As I stared at her in disbelief, she rode up and asked if there was a good place to crash and to take a shower. The principal arrived and told her that she could crash where we were staying and use the shower. After she cleaned herself up and got some food, she explained the purpose of her journey.

She was just riding. No goal, no destination, no designated length of time. Just riding. She must have been searching for something. However, when you think about it, she had freedom. What she was doing takes a lot of guts, to totally cut yourself off from the outside world and just ride. She left a few days later and I was still awestruck. That is probably one of the most intense things I have seen someone do. She was rather casual about it all. I suddenly felt childish for being hesitant to disappear for a few days to a mates place.

I hope she found what she was looking for. That girl was stronger and had more determination than I and a lot of other folks ever will. She was also definitely fitter than I'll ever be (I really should go to the gym). I emailed her a few years later, to see how she was progressing. She is now living on a small island with her child. From what I could gather, she seemed happy in her new location. Life takes twists and turns, we just have to learn to enjoy the ride.

Fishing

One day, the principal of the school I was teaching at took the other student teachers and I out for a fishing trip. We got into his car, a 4WD of some sort, with the back seats facing the sides of the vehicle rather than the front. Like you see in the back of those army trucks. The guy was smiling the whole time as he drove us to our destination. Knowing that he was a bit of a prankster, I was very suspicious. He was not an angry guy and was great with the school children, but the look on his face that day was one of pure joy. Eventually, he pulled over and stopped at a gate leading to a paddock. I guessed the river was nearby.

It was not. Not even close. However, what was near was a bunch of hills, bumps and other wonderful obstructions in our way. That smile on the face of the principal got wider. We got through the gate, he closed it behind us and then he began to drive. He started to accelerate and the bumps hit us. My backside was still sore from that injury to the coccus. That next half hour of driving was excruciating. The demonic smile that the principal had never stopped shining. I felt that he had a little too much fun with that adventure.

Eventually he parked the car and let us out. I was still shaking for a good minute or two after. He handed us each a rod and sent us down to the river. He gave me a few instructions on what to do, checked the area to make sure it was all safe and then went to a different spot to try his luck.

We didn't have bait, yet, we did have lures. I was standing there for a long time, sending the line sailing into the water again and again. I almost managed to catch a fish. I could see it in the water, it was so clear. It was a kind of long fish, about forty centimetres in length and I almost had it. However, at the last moment, as I continued to reel it in, it broke free. The sun reflected off the scales and it swam away for freedom. This was one of my only real great fishing experiences, but I think it's better this way. I don't even like fish anyway.

The principal did catch a fish in the end and he and the others ate well that night.

It hurts

In the final days before my departure, I finally gained the trust of the kids in my class. This is notoriously hard to do, given the history between the European and Aboriginal people. Understandably so, the trust of westerners is generally not readily given.

One day, I noticed a huge boil on one of the kid's arms. It looked nasty and I was worried. I asked if he had seen the doctor, to which he replied, "Nope." It seemed, from the red colour and oozing wound, to be rather infected. I told him, "You should definitely go. There is a risk of it getting much worse." Still, he refused to see the doctor. I'm not sure if it was purely a macho act from the kid or if it is a lingering inherited fear from the earlier times where children were taken away from their parents. Either way, he wasn't interested in going. Doctors are something many of the Aboriginal people in the outback seem unwilling to utilise unless it is a grave matter. Fear or no fear, that kid had to get to a doctor soon or he might have ended up losing the whole arm. Finally, he suggested, "I will go see the doctor. But only if you come along with me." I promised that I would, and so he agreed.

When we arrived, the doctor took a look and gently covered the boil with a bandage to stop it getting damaged and to prevent any more debris entering the wound. She also gave him tablets to combat the infection within the boil. However, he still said it hurt. So she gave him a sling for his arm to help restrict any movement of his arm. She messed up the first one and went to put the bandage in the bin. He asked if he could have it. "Why not", she replied, it was that or the rubbish bin. A few more attempts and we were on our way out, heading back out towards the school.

Once we arrived outside, he stopped, put the bandage on his foot and one around his head and then limped into class. All the kids were looking at him with great concern. He seemed pretty happy with himself. I am not sure if he took the tablets. I did, however, see the bandage on his leg and arm for a good few days after that. He was playing football and it didn't seem to hurt so bad anymore. Soon after that, I had to leave.

On the way back up north to Darwin, after leaving the town, dust filling my rear view mirror and leaving such a different life behind, I was stuck in thought. I was very sad to say goodbye to such an amazing bunch of human beings. It was also going to be a challenging transition to go back to the city life I was used to living. I had to go back to attending my university class the next day, where everyone would be looking to me for answers. They wanted to know how we could deal with the indigenous people and help them through a difficult patch in their history. I wasn't sure how to answer. Honestly, I am still not.

Whatever we are doing is not working, however, I am not sure what the right thing is. I hope we can find it and these people can get what they are looking for to be at peace. Perhaps, a good start could be involving the indigenous people in the discussion of how the legislation should represent the people.

I thought this was supposed to help

A few years later I was lucky enough to visit another part in the north of Australia called Cairns. This time, instead of going for work, I was there on holiday. I was fortunate enough to not be alone and a tall red-headed girl, by the name of Heidi, would be joining me on the trip. The weather was similar to Darwin, except it has rain forests and access to the Great Barrier Reef. The biological nerd in me went crazy. We were going to be staying there for five days.

The first full day was booked to take a snorkel trip in the Great Barrier Reef. I had heard so many stories from people who had been before. I was able to set goals, based on the awesome adventures of others. I wanted to find a sea turtle and Nemo.

After a few hours flying out from Melbourne we landed and took a taxi to our hotel. Heidi and I had a little walk around the town, booked a few more adventures and then found food before calling it a night. There is a reasonably strong party scene in Cairns, but that just isn't my thing.

As I said, the day finally arrived where we would visit the big reef. We arrived at the pier from where our boat would be leaving. The boat for the voyage would be the 'Passions of Paradise' catamaran. It was beautiful weather, with clear sunny skies. People were waiting around for the boat to arrive and you could see the excitement in everyone's eyes. It was going to be a long boat ride on a catamaran to arrive at the part of the outer reef we were to visit. On the way to the destination, Heidi and I were informed of what to do and not to do while swimming in the reef.

Normally, I don't get seasick. However, after reading about the rough waters in the area, and a couple of recommendations on Tripadvisor, I decided that with all the neat things to see I was not going to take any chances. I popped a sea sickness tablet I had purchased earlier, in a last minute rush to a local pharmacy. For the first hour or so it seemed to work well. Then, out of nowhere, I started getting stomach cramps. It was not cool. I tried to hide it from everyone because I really wanted to swim, but it just got worse and worse. I went through a list of things I had done the day before. Had I eaten anything weird? No. Had I drunk from any weird water sources? No. Could I have eaten something I was allergic to? Possibly. There is always a risk of contamination when you have death by gluten syndrome. I looked at the packet of sea

The Other Side Of Travelling

sickness tablets to check I had done it all right. Had I taken the wrong dose? Did I take it too late? Was there any weird side effects that I hadn't seen? No. The answer was much more straightforward.

Again, in my excitement I hadn't thought things through. I am allergic to gluten and the tablet had gluten which worked as a binding agent or something. So, in an attempt to stop myself from getting sick, I made myself sick. Rookie mistake and one I determined I would never make again. You will read sentences to this effect throughout the book. I always have good intentions, however, I have a terrible habit of making myself sick wherever I go.

However, as the boat ride was rather long, by the time Heidi and I finally arrived at the first location, I was well enough to dive. Still queasy, but "not one second away from throwing up" ill.

The first location was near a small island. The water wasn't deep and it was warm. The island itself was not very interesting. It looked more like a small sand dune, was rather spare of vegetation, but looked very like it belonged there. As I jumped off the ladder of the boat and was diving into the beautiful, clear salty water of our location, I looked back. A good third of the passengers on the boat would not be joining us for the swim. They were all smashed by seasickness. It seemed like an emergency ward. They were lying on the ground, or hanging loosely from chairs. Their faces were beaded with sweat and a grey colour tinged their skin. Their movements were feeble. I thought they must be so bummed out to not be going in. But, as I caught eyes with one, I understood. They didn't care about going in anymore. They felt so terrible, they just wanted that feeling to stop. I felt now that I had to enjoy it more for them too. Heidi jumped in right behind me.

There was much life swimming around in that reef. There were giant clams, rainbow coloured fish, coral existing in a variety of shapes and sizes. The animals did not give a single damn that we were there. They mostly just looked confused at us. They swam around, doing their business. One parrotfish started gnawing at a rock nearby me. My underwater camera picked up the sound.

As amazing as everything was, I noticed as I swam around how so much damage to the reef had been done already. Bleaching is taking a real effect.

Getting used to the snorkel took a while, yet, soon I was diving and swimming around. I even found Nemo. No sea turtle though unfortunately. I noticed a second reason for the less than healthy appearance of certain aspects of this reef. Stupid tourists standing on coral. The good people on the ship had instructed us to be extremely careful not to damage the coral in the reef. Some people, however, just need to destroy an organism to get the perfect selfie. It still makes me angry, just thinking about it.

The second location was rougher, but still lovely. It was in the middle of the ocean. There was no land in sight, but when we dived in to the water, there was a rock formation roughly one hundred metres across. It felt a lot colder, due to the distance from land. Yet, it still had plenty of wildlife to be seen. I tried to take as many clear photos to show my grandparents when I got back. However, try as I might, unfortunately I couldn't hold still in the choppy water. The waves kept lifting me up and down just as I was taking a photo, making the whole shot blurry. In the end, I gave up and gave the camera to Heidi. She did a far better job with the photos. I tried swimming with a school of fish.

I will have to go back there one day to see a sea turtle. I hope I can find one. As I just mentioned, I had hired an underwater camera to take all the epic snaps of my travels. I must say, it was not worth it. All the photos and video were almost useless.

I hope this giant ecosystem manages to stay around. It is too cool to lose.

Bart and Elmo

The next day, after the reef trip, Heidi and I took a bus tour. Usually, I don't like to do bus tours. In fact, normally, I hate them with a passion. They are so rigid that it can often feel like you missed out on something. They leave you feeling as if you should see a lot more. Or even worse, they give you the feeling that you saw too much of something you wish you could have left out. However, given my time frame, my choices were rather limited. I was a man on a mission and wanted to see as much as I could with the time I had. Hiring a car and driving around looking for locations would have wasted too much time.

We got onto the bus and immediately knew it was going to be an exciting day. The tour guide introduced himself as "Bart". He had a bald patch, about the size of a Pringles lid. The rest of his hair was tied back into a long white ponytail. He wore no shoes. The street must have been fifty degrees Celsius. I don't know how his skin wasn't peeling as he stood there calmly on the asphalt. Maybe they had already turned to leather? He was also a larger gentleman, but seemed very nimble on his feet.

He closed the door and then got into the driver's seat. He turned around, said a quick "Hi", and checked to make sure everyone on the bus was meant to be there and had paid. Once all the business side of things had been taken care off, the fun began. He proceeded to pull out a stuffed toy Elmo from somewhere in the front compartment. He introduced Elmo to us. A few people weakly said "Hello." There was a small exchange of looks amongst the passengers. What had we signed up for? Bart looked a little disappointed at the reception of his close, red, fluffy friend. He continued though, and explained that, "Elmo was around in case anyone needed a hug or anything. Elmo always listens and never criticises. If you need help, just ask Elmo or myself and we will do all they can to assist you."

When the introduction of our guide and soft toy companion was out of the way, we were off. Heidi and I exchanged looks of confusion. I was not sure if I felt comfortable being in the car with this guy anymore. What if Elmo told him to drive off a cliff? How much power over Bart did Elmo have? Who was really in control? All these things concerned me.

The first stop on this tour was a nearby forest and we saw a number of unique trees. I know, trees are a significant part of any rainforest and that previous sentence was somewhat redundant. However, these specific trees were different.

There is a parasitic tree that grows in this particular forest. The fruit is eaten by birds. Then, the faeces drops onto the leaves in the upper canopy as the bird flies away. The seeds in the poop starts growing and growing down towards the ground. Slowly, it keeps growing strands and branches until it reaches the soil far down below. Digging this line deep in and tapping into the water supply and with the support of the tree that is now its host, it continues to increase in size. Branches continue to grow in every direction, surrounding the host tree. Eventually the whole of the host plant inside is strangled by the surrounding branches of the parasitic tree. The inside of the plant rots away, leaving only the parasite behind. Basically, what this means is that you can step inside the tree and look around inside the hollow. It was super weird.

Bart next took us to a waterfall. We went for a swim. Then Bart wanted us all in turn to re-enact that famous advertisement. You know, the one where the lady whips her hair back creating an arch of water with the waterfall behind her? The shampoo ad. One by one we all re-enacted that. As far as I was concerned, I looked particularly beautiful, but, for some reason the photo never got saved.

We went to a few other locations, with Bart turning out to be a great guy, knowledgeable and passionate for the environment. He wasn't even that crazy and he really knew his stuff. On our way back to Cairns, there was one final stop. It was definitely the coolest. There were platypi in the area. Until now, neither Heidi or I had managed to see one in the wild. However, by the end of that tour, it was something else that we could tick off our list.

They are such beautiful creatures. Some stupid tourist used a flash camera, scaring them away, but I got a glimpse before that happened. After this, Bart and Elmo took us home. On the way back, I had the chance to talk to Bart a little more. He genuinely cares about the environment and seemed to think that if he could show people the impressive locations out there, they might help protect it. I don't know about the others, but what I saw sure convinced me to start changing how my actions impacted the environment. It was an interesting day. And no, Elmo didn't tell him to drive off the cliff, to which I am thankful.

Hold Me, I'm Scared

We took another bus trip going to another famous rainforest the next day. I think from memory, it was the Daintree rainforest. There were again, of course, epic trees and other wildlife. But, while on tour, there was one thing that I saw that I will never forget.

As part of the scheduled tour, we stopped at a beach. It looked like any other beach. It was a large sandy area, the waves were rolling in gently, the smell of salt filled the air. For most people, this is a dream location. However, beaches are generally not for me. So, not being a fan of those, I decided to look around in the forest behind the dunes. There was a pathway into the forest and so, Heidi and I began to explore. Along the way, we saw a lot of bush turkeys and other birds of sorts flapping around in the dead leaves and other debris.

One particular bush turkey was rather enterprising. It was apparently taking full advantage of the fact that it was a tourist spot. With nothing much to threaten them, they had become quite bold. A couple of the people on our tour were eating food at a wooden table nearby. The bird naturally jumped up and started going for it. The people screamed, but did not much else. The bird had a great feast. Heidi and I had a good laugh. It is not often that mother nature scores a point back against the humans. However, here was a good example of her ability to win one for Team Environment. Heidi remarked that, "This particular bush turkey looks mighty plump. In another time, it probably would have easily been caught, killed and eaten for a nice dinner." Clearly, Heidi was getting hungry, so we moved along.

We followed the boardwalk path for about ten minutes. As we walked past a clearing in the forest, we heard a scraping sound. At first, we couldn't exactly pinpoint where it was coming from. It wasn't loud and one quick scan of our surroundings told us that there was no bush turkeys in the area. Heidi and I continued to look around, slightly creeped out by our inability to identify where the noise came from. Finally, we discovered the sound was coming from something moving under the leaves. It was coming towards us. We were both rather wary, considering the possibility that it was a snake or some other creature not worth messing with. Most of Australia is not worth messing with. When it finally appeared through the leaves and on to the walking platform, it was far creepier than I could have imagined.

First a large wasp-like creature, orange in colour, broke through the vegetation, crawling along the ground. It was walking backwards. We immediately stepped back. Orange like that means danger and I was not going to play a game of chicken with it. It still didn't make sense though. We looked at each other with confusion, it was not big enough to be making the noises we heard. Heidi turned to me and asked, "Why is it walking backwards though?"

As its head cleared the leaves though, we could see it was dragging something. Something big. Much bigger than itself. It was a species of spider, hairy and on its back with its legs in the air at funny angles. The wasp was dragging it along the ground and taking it somewhere. Personally, I did not want to be a part of that. Heidi, while curious about the organism itself, was not that excited about getting too close either. So, we left and went back to the group at the beach.

When we caught up again with the main group, I asked the tour guide what the wasp was doing. He explained that, "The spider was likely still alive. This species of wasp actually paralyses it and then drags it back to a nest where it lays eggs. The spider will be the feast of the baby wasps as they come out. The spider will likely still be alive when that happens."

It's OK, when I heard that, it took me a while to get to sleep too. If you want to look up more info, it is called the Orange Spider Wasp. A very creative name, I know. Australia either uses rhyming slang, where the actual meaning is at least three degrees of separation from the word said, or it is so unimaginatively named that you can't tell if they are actually joking.

After that, the guide helped everyone to pack up and we went back on our way. I hope I never meet anything like that wasp again anytime soon.

The interesting fruit

The last major activity Heidi and I did in Cairns was to go up by cable car with a glass bottom to a small town called Kuranda. Kuranda sits in some mountains that appear to come up out of nowhere, close to the shore.

The journey up the mountain was amazing, with a memorable view. In fact, it was so picturesque, that even with my fear of heights, I couldn't help looking at the lush forest just beneath my feet. Even if you decide not to take the cable car, there is one thing you must do and that is to take the tour through the forest there. There is an Aboriginal guide that takes you through and explains a bit of the history of the area as well as showing you what plants can and cannot be eaten. They also show you some of the traditional aspects of indigenous life. It was really a hidden gem. In fact, it was so unknown that we were the only two on the tour. Bad for the tour. Great for me. Score.

The tour guide we had was a guy named Aaron. He was young, probably early twenties and a little nervous. He had short black hair, a loose grey shirt on and was also wearing some cargo shorts. We would be his first ever customers. Every time he was interrupted by his radio or one of the million questions from me, he would repeat the same script to get back to his point. After a while and a bombardment of questions to prove our interest, we managed to get him off script and into real experiences. There was some cool insights there and seeing his face as we triggered childhood memories of fishing and swimming in rivers was pretty nice.

One thing on that tour that I found fascinating was that, there are supposedly two very special fruit in that forest. One gives you epic diarrhoea, so severe, I wouldn't be surprised if you got airborne from the propulsion of the release. The other constipates better than a diet of white toast and banana. I find it funny to imagine how the first person discovered these properties.

I find it even more amusing to think of people that got the fruit mixed up in the middle of the night, looking for a snack. You can picture it right? It's dark, the moon isn't up. The fruit is about the same size, you can't see, but you are starving. You grab a couple from the basket and munch away. You wake up to the discovery that you made a huge mistake. There must have been a lot of trial and error to work out the balance to not be affected. A false move meant a bad day for the eater. Actually, a false move could mean a bad day for the tribe. Imagine if you were the cook and put the wrong fruit in. You would have a lot of cleaning up to do.

Overall, Cairns was an exceptional place to visit. The only real minus was a pair of the most useless pick-pocketers I ever saw. I mean, that gives you the indication of how bad they were. We saw them. You shouldn't see a pick-pocketer ever.

Anyway, it was late at night and Heidi and I were walking

back to the hotel. There were two guys, one on each side of the street. They saw us and each looking at one another, stood up, and started to follow. Every time we turned back, they pretended to look at a store. They continued following us. So, we turned around and smiled at them. Heidi even gave a small wave. They immediately froze. Very slowly they turned around and walked away. You could almost hear them blaming one another for being noticed.

It doesn't matter where you are, keep your head on a swivel so you don't get or find yourself in a bad situation. Don't get caught out by idiots like that.

You know what you are doing, right?

A couple of years ago, in between all this travelling, I decided to try and do the right thing by donating blood. It seemed like it was a win-win for everyone involved. Someone got my blood and I got lots of chocolate milk at the end. What further argument was needed? The first few times I went, it went OK, but something about the angle of the needle or how my arm was lying meant that the blood was coming out a little slower than they would have liked. After a certain time frame they have to stop taking the blood so they can start the storing process. They sucked what they could from me and let me go.

The fourth time I came in though, was different. I got into the big reclining chair and the nurse went about completing the standard tests. She checked that my iron levels were not too low for the procedure. She checked my blood pressure. After all this, she explained that they had an apprentice with them today. The nurse asked, "Would it be OK if you became her practice patient for today?" What I thought in my head, was that I was going to be the practice pin cushion. However, I agreed. They have to learn somehow, right?

I could clearly see she was nervous, so I tried to calm her down by having a chat with her beforehand. "Look", I said, "I have lots of tattoos and have done this plenty of times. Me and needles are OK, you have nothing to worry about." She smiled at me and continued to look nervous.

The first sign that I maybe should have used as an excuse to pull out of being the human pin cushion was that she spilt the disinfectant they put on your arm before beginning. Such a simple task failed did not bode well for the more complex aspect to come. Still, I didn't want to disappoint. I let her continue. After the disinfectant finally made it on my arm, she got the needle hooked up to the bag and was ready to begin.

Her hands were shaking. It looked like she was playing one of those arcade games with my arm. You know the ones, where there is something going from left to right on the screen and you need to press a button so that it drops in the middle to make the tower higher? Yeah, she did that with my arm. Just like the game too, where for some reason, everyone who plays assumes that if you hit the button harder, the mechanism drops quicker, she smashed that needle into my arm.

It hurt. Like really hurt. It felt like my whole arm was on fire or something. However, she was smiling at me, figuring she had done a good job. Blood was trickling into the bag. I decided to be stupid, take one for the team and boost her confidence by not saying anything. I figured the sooner she was calm, the sooner she would be OK. I hoped that I would be OK.

So I let her go and sat there. My arm was still in pain. The blood was flowing. How could it not, with a puncture like that? About halfway through, I started to feel a little faint. However, I was determined to fill the bag this time. I was pulling a fist again and again to help pump the blood out. The nurse came back, checked the bag, asked me a few questions and then took the needle out. However, even though the needle was gone, my arm continued to tingle. I smiled at her as best I could and said she did a great job. My insides were swirling at this point. I wanted to throw up. It had never been like this before. But, I decided that the show must go on. At which point I stood up to try and get away to show how successfully she had done her job.

Instead, I dropped to the floor and fainted. I think I didn't boost her confidence as much as I would have liked. I was dragged by her and another old nurse to a couch, where I was force-fed sweets and chocolate milk and water and whatever else they could give me. Eventually, I was OK enough to leave and drive home. I probably didn't drink enough water on the hot summer's day before the process of donating started.

As a secondary consequence for being stupid, my arm tingled for the next six weeks as the nerve she had accidentally damaged healed. Imagine your funny bone being hit constantly for six weeks and you get the idea. It was probably still worth it. All the same, I don't recommend following my example. The stupid part I mean. Do give blood, that is awesome and helps people.

The Evil Penguin

Look, I'll be honest. I love nature. I studied Biology. I am all about saving the environment and protecting the endangered species and such. I think we are screwing up a lot of things that we have no right to touch. However, I am not so naive to think that it is all innocent animals and evil humans. I come from Australia, so I have seen what little arseholes animals can be. Take this story for example.

There is a place about an hour's drive out from Melbourne called Phillip Island. It is a nice place to visit and has a number of small-town attractions. Chocolate stores, little souvenir shops, and cheesy t-shirt selling establishments. But, most people who make their way down there go there to see a particular species of penguin. When I was growing up they used to be called the "fairy penguins". They have since been rebranded as the "little penguins" for political reasons. They are pretty small. The name makes sense.

The set up at the sanctuary works something like this. The people line up and sit on a raised platform at the edge of the beach. You have to be there well before sunset. They shut down the roads at a certain point. The penguins come home every night after feeding, in groups. They normally arrive just as the sun comes down. They spook easily though, so flashes from cameras, for example, would be enough for them to scurry back into the water. When they arrive, they run up the beach to the right of the platform and make a mad dash for their nests.

I went there to check it out. On the day I went, it was cold but clear weather. Just as predicted, around sunset there was a small mass of penguins gathered in the water, just beyond the shallow area. They were waiting for the coast to be clear. Eventually, a small group of about ten surfaced at the edge of the breaking waves and started to waddle cautiously up the beach. As is typical in many such situations, there are always a few that think that the "rule" of no flash applies to everyone else except them. So a few people, using their thousand times zoom, took some shots from their cameras. The flash stopped the penguins halfway up the beach. There was immediate panic in the group. The group dispersed. Four ran in a mad dash towards the sand dunes, while the other six went for the surf. A calm attendant, in a tired, apathetic voice, reminded the tourists that the no flash rule applied to everyone.

After about ten minutes, the penguins plucked up their courage for a second attempt. This time, they came up with reinforcements. Around twenty surfaced and made their way up in a tight-knit group. It was cold without the sun, and the people who had used their flash before were clearly ready to leave, as they already had their photographic evidence. However, they had to wait for the penguins to make their way up so as not to disturb the process. After a decent percentage of the little penguin population were up in the dunes, squawking at one another and waddling around, we were allowed to go and follow groups of penguins from raised boardwalks as they made their way towards their nests. My friend and I found a group that seemed to be interesting, and started following them quietly.

There was a group of around seven coming up to a small secluded section which was away from most tourists. Two of them were fighting. I am unfamiliar with the rules in penguin boxing, but I guess one lost and was left behind as a punishment. He scurried under the boardwalk for safety, hiding in the darkness. The rest of the group left. They didn't even look back. It was pretty harsh. The little chirping under the boardwalk broke our hearts.

We were feeling sorry for our abandoned friend when we saw a new group of penguins coming up the pathway between the dunes. We kept our fingers crossed and hoped that our webbed companion would soon be accepted into the new club. He wasn't and we soon found out why.

The abandoned penguin waited under the walkway until most of the group had passed. As soon as he was in line with the slow stragglers of the group, he shot out like a bullet and started attacking one of them. I stared with my mouth open. I couldn't believe what I was seeing. It was a bully penguin. Soon enough the group walked away and he returned to his hiding place.

The next group came along and sure enough, the hidden penguin waited and ambushed. It shot out as fast as lightning at the last penguins, introduced chaos and disorder, before he made a small grunting noise and returned to his post. We had found our first penguin troll. If there was a penguin version of YouTube, he would be the guy in the comments ripping apart music videos for music genres he hates. He attacked and returned again and again. I could not work out why. It didn't seem to give him any benefit. I searched my head for selective pressures that would have had a penguin evolve in such a matter. Generally, a group is an important survival strategy for penguins, so to be a loner is not a good idea. So, why it was isolating itself is perplexing.

I wanted to find out whether that behaviour was normal, but the staff were preoccupied trying to stop half the other tourists from shooting flashing lights brighter than the sun into the eyes of the poor penguins. I figured that my question could wait and continued to watch the spectacle. If I had to think of a name for that little penguin, it would be something like "Trolling Beak". I know it's not creative, but it is descriptive and gets the point across quickly. It would be a warning for the other penguins not to cross it. I like to think he is out there still, every night, fighting the system like a little punk penguin, trolling the world.

We left the park once all the penguins were safely home again and we were allowed to drive again. We were told to check under our cars for hidden penguins and to drive slowly. We made it back to the hotel and headed back to Melbourne the next day.

A relaxing holiday, he said.

For my honeymoon, I went on a trip to the southern island of Australia called Tasmania. However, it was not just me and my wife going on my honeymoon. My wife's friends, Sacha, Hanna and Christiane, who had all travelled all the way from Germany would be coming for the few days that they had remaining in Australia, in order to check out the tourist spots. While it was not an ideal situation, the people were cool and they had helped out a lot with the wedding, so the least we could do was to show them some of the more beautiful places to visit in the south of Australia.

The day before we left, we visited Healesville Sanctuary and got to hang out with a wombat. It was pretty cool and the animals themselves are very interesting creatures. They are generally lazy and sleep almost all the time, but if trouble comes, they can really defend themselves. They have a bony plate in their lower back which they can use like a hydraulic press. The dog enters the burrow, the wombat backs up and raises its backside, crushing the skulls between the roof of the burrow and the plate. I think that sums up Australia pretty

The Other Side Of Travelling

well. Cute, fluffy, sleepy, and violent. For our visit, all it did was eat grass and look awesome. I suppose it did try to eat Christiane's shoes, because they were green, but otherwise, it was all good.

The next day, we flew out super early. We left the house at about 4 am. Some of the people on the trip were not what you would call "morning people", but they made a big effort and we all managed to get into the car without being late.

For some reason or another, the day that we were flying out, the airport car space was full. I have never seen it that bad in my life. We had booked a parking space in advance. We still struggled to find a park as the time got closer and closer to our designated flight departure. With only thirty minutes to go, we managed to find a spot, parked the car and proceeded to get our luggage out. I should say, most of us. Sacha could not find his luggage in the car. It was not clear how, but somehow, in the chaos, his stuff was left behind.

With so little time before the flight departure, we decided to sort out the luggage problem in Hobart. The flight itself was smooth and when we landed, we began the task of assembling an emergency holiday kit for our friend. There were the standards, such as clothes and toiletries. These could be found cheaply at Kmart. The killer for the budget, however, was the tobacco. Sacha had heard the legends of how much cigarettes cost in Australia before he came and so brought with him some cheap ones from Europe. They were all left in the luggage back in Melbourne, so he would have to buy Australian. For the cheap price of fifty dollars, he received what would have cost roughly a fifth of the price back in Europe. He got a bonus picture of a blood clot in a lung taken from a dead person with his purchase. For some reason, he didn't seem too appreciative of this deluxe bonus gift. This was not a good start to the trip.

It got even better once I realised that I had perhaps not been quite clear with the plan for the trip. I had explained that we were taking a flight to Tasmania, an island off the coast of

Australia. I also explained that we would drive from Hobart to a mountain and stay the night there in a cabin. What I failed to factor in, was the difference in what is considered a small distance for a European as opposed to an Australian.

We piled into the rented vehicle and I cheerfully explained that we were now only four hours away from our destination. The guests in my car all looked like they had been hit by a freight train. I asked them if everything was OK, to which they all replied, "Fine." Their tone of voice did not suggest fine, and I found out that the idea of that long a drive after a flight, just to get to the location was not what they had pictured as a short holiday. I assured them that it would all be worth it when we got to see Cradle Mountain and all the wildlife. After that, the crew cheered up and the drive up was pleasant.

We stopped off at some caves to see some glow worms. They were cool. The walk to the caves through a forest was also nice and gave everyone a chance to stretch their legs. Finally, after a very long day, we arrived at our cabin at around 5 pm. The gang was a bit sceptical as they got out of the car. I had promised wildlife, and so far, the only animals they had seen were the dead potoroos every five hundred metres on the side of the road. Yet as we looked out the window of our cabin at dusk, we saw wildlife everywhere. Everyone was so happy to see the little animals doing their thing, that they forgot about the tension of the day.

After darkness fell, we took a drive to the Tasmanian Devil Sanctuary and learned about the conservation efforts being made to stop this awesome animal from becoming extinct. They have a cancer that is contagious due to a genetic closeness in the population. They are trying breeding programs to get the devils back to full strength. They are nocturnal and make plenty of noise. Really cute animals, when they are not eating and/or fighting. If you want to see footage of this cool animal, the best I can think of is the Wild Boyz video on the animals. Maybe you can find it online. If not, I'm sure David At-

The Other Side Of Travelling

tenborough has probably covered it somewhere. He has done everything.

We visited every part of the zoo before heading out. After the night zoo, we headed back to the cabin and, after a failed attempt on my part to start a fire, we decided to call it a night and fall asleep.

The next day we got up bright and early, as we were going to tackle Cradle Mountain. It was sunny, but there was a little bit of cloud in the air. We drove the half an hour required to get to the location, got out of the car and looked at the amazing landscape. The view was amazing. The lake was reflecting a beautiful picture of the mountain in the water, creating one of those cool mirror images. There were a few clouds in the sky, but it was picturesque, not grey sky or anything. I had a big smile on my face. This was one of my dreams coming true. I was so excited. I turned to my companions to see how excited they were and I saw a familiar look on their faces.

My wife was fine, but the rest showed a different thought process. Excitement would not accurately describe the emotion that was portrayed. Hanna asked, "Um...How long is the hike?" I told her, "It is a nice, little, seven-hour return trip." I reasoned, "You will get a great chance to enjoy some real Australian wilderness." As the group collectively dropped their jaws, I could see that either, I had not made it clear or the companions couldn't really believe that this was what we would choose to do for a honeymoon activity. To their credit, they recovered quickly and brought back their enthusiasm.

However, the positive feelings did not last long, as we started to leave the nice lake track and make the ascent to the peak. My wife and I were prepared. Christiane had the right clothing at least, but was seriously lacking in supplies. Hanna and Sacha were totally unprepared and inadequately equipped for a challenge of this type. They quickly bowed out and returned to the nice lake track where they had an enjoyable time taking in the sights and scenery from the lake.

My wife, Christiane and I remained on the mountain path

and used the chains embedded into the rock to help pull us up the steep track. Eventually, we reached a point where it was flat for quite a while. It seemed that the mountain was like two giant steps. There was a steep rise from the lake to where we had just arrived, a long flat stretch and then a steep rocky climb again to the pinnacle. We took the opportunity on the flat section to recover, have some water and food as well as get our breath back. As previously stated, due to my lack of clear explanation of the plan, Christiane did not bring much in the way of food or water. So, we shared some of ours with her. We reached the base of the second steep section around three hours in, slowly making our way up.

When I was almost at the top, my phone started ringing. I had set an alarm for three and a half hours. This was to ensure that we had enough time to come back. This is an old habit of mine. I had decided that wherever we were, when this alarm went off, the hike was finished and it was time to return. So, with the pinnacle in sight and not far off, we turned around and made our way back down to the base of the second steep section.

Here we had a choice. We could return the way we came, or turn right and follow another path back down. We were feeling pretty adventurous after what we had just achieved. We opted for the variety and turned right.

For a long time, this seemed like the better choice. The road gradually sloped down and continued for some time without too much difficulty. We had good views of the lake below. However, as we came around a bend, we saw the first of our troubles. The way down from this point was super steep. In fact, if it wasn't for the chains provided, it would have taken a very long time to get down. There was not much choice. So, pushing forward, we began and made the deliberately slow movements down the mountain.

At some point, the lack of water and food intake started to mess with the endurance of all of us, but more so our friend. Her legs were shaking and she was not doing so well. As she moved, using the chain as a guide around one of the corners, she slipped. She was holding on and as she had made a habit of not looking down to see how high up she was, she did not panic. I, afraid of heights and in full view of the situation, was indeed panicking. I looked to my wife, who had gone before Christiane and I, and her face told me that she was panicking too.

I told my friend to hold on. I, slowly coming down the chain, helped her put her feet right, as casually as possible. I smiled at her, she continued down the path and I sighed for relief. She would have seriously injured herself if she had made one false move. But, she didn't and all was fine. The rest of the way down, she made it just fine though and when we got to the bottom, we celebrated our success. For someone who was underprepared for the situation, she really kicked butt and never gave up. If someone had sprung a seven-hour hike on me as a surprise, I would probably have thrown a tantrum and sulked.

We found the Sacha and Hanna at the car park. We took the car back to the cabin. Along the way, we swapped stories. It was a good day in the end, but we were all very sore.

The next day, we took the car and drove back to Hobart, stopping off at Russell Falls with the hope of catching sight of a platypus. We were unsuccessful.

We got to the hotel in Hobart and had a good sleep. In the morning, I woke up and asked if anyone was in to see some examples of some of the oldest trees in the world, the Huon Pine. They were popular for shipbuilding because they have a chemical that effectively stops rotting. However, they were over-forested, and it takes a long time for them to grow back, so they are now somewhat protected.

My wife, having studied biology, was in. I can't understand why, but the others said that they might just have a rest day. I guess people have different styles of travel. Perhaps I was a little mean to them with my travel itinerary. I have had to learn that what I call a "relaxing time" is not the same as other peoples' idea of a relaxing time. What I call "chilled", others call "torture".

My wife and I took the car and we drove down to the reserve. It was a nice day, but quite foggy when we first arrived. We still got to see some amazing wildlife, including some black cockatoos. I highly recommend checking it out. We even found some of the pines, which was great.

On the way back, we stopped off at a random Orchard. My favourite fruit is apples and my favourite alcoholic drink is cider. I don't drink often, but when I do, cider is invariably my beverage of choice. It hence made sense for me to check it out. I would find apples and maybe, if I was very lucky, I would perhaps find some cool cider to try.

I pulled in and talked to a worker sorting out apples out the front of the barn. She was a middle-aged lady, slender with her hair tied back. I explained the situation and what I was looking for. They were more than able to provide. By coincidence, I had not bumped into a random worker, but rather the owner of the orchard. They took us around the back and showed us some wine-shaped bottles which were unlabelled. We bought some apples and some of the dodgy unlabelled cider and took it back to the hotel.

We opened it up and tried it. It was the best cider I had ever had. Somewhat between a dry wine and a cider, it was exactly the sort of thing I had been looking for. I have not been able to find anything quite the same since. I am not really a drinker of alcohol, but this stuff was very, very nice. The closest was an apple wine in Germany, but it didn't quite match the lightness. We called the owner up and asked if it was possible to get some more. She said yes and directed us to the online store. These bottles looked way more legit. It seemed she had given us some that were not yet labelled. So our first thoughts about the dodgy bottle were not so well founded. Once again, by being open and spontaneous to things and events coming my way, I met cool people and had a wonderful experience.

On the last day, we went to the famous market of Hobart,

called Salamanca Market. It had lots of different produce. Sadly there was a lot of produce made out of the Huon pine, but one cool find that I can recommend for you all was solid shampoo bars. I bought a couple and have not gone back since. Especially when travelling, these are handy as they don't leak and because they are not liquid, you don't have to worry about them when travelling light and only taking carry-on luggage. This saved me a lot of trouble at the airport. I have enough trouble at airports anyway with so-called "random checks".

We flew back the next day to Melbourne and our friends spent the last few days chilling and recovering after the intense trip. I'm guessing that next time, they will pick the travel itinerary.

It's a beautiful view. What is it?

One of the last trips I did before I left to my new home in Germany was to visit the Grampians in Victoria, Australia. The idea was to get a cabin and do some hiking, as well as, hopefully show my wife some of the native animals in their natural habitat. It was me, my wife, and a British friend of ours, Nick, that made the journey out. On the way there, I drove and we arrived at our cabin around 2 pm.

I have to admit that the weather wasn't great; it was May and the whole sky was overcast. However, as soon as we arrived, we saw at least thirty kangaroos lying around the place. They were just chilling, as if it was normal. I guess it was a normal thing at one point, before cities came along. There was also a substantial flock of emus (are they called a flock, a group, a murder, a whatever of emus?). I proudly turned to my wife and explained that, as promised, here you could see some of the most famous Australian wildlife. My wife was laughing. Nick was having a quiet chuckle too. I couldn't understand why. Were the animals doing something funny? Were they doing something naughty?

Once they gained control again, my wife answered my questioning with a question. She asked me, "Have you seen all the natural, indigenous, Australian deer that are over to the right?" I had not. It seems that there is a population of European Deer that now live in the area. My partner had grown up seeing them, but I had not, so this was a new experience for me. However, all the native wilderness lost a bit of its shine after that. The point was to get to see the real Australia, but it was better than nothing.

We stayed the night there in a comfortable log cabin with a nice fire helping to fight the cold. To pass the time, we played Monopoly – I won of course (and even if I didn't, it's my book, my story, I write it, so I am the winner. Just don't ask Nick). Then we had an early night as we planned to take a hike to a beautiful vantage point called "the Pinnacle" that I had heard of.

We woke up the next day, had a quick breakfast and set off bright and early. Although it was cloudy, we had hopes that the view would make it all worthwhile. On the way up, there were some cool rock formations, as well as some interesting flora and fauna all around. For some reason though, I did get the peculiar feeling that the roof was closing in. This was especially weird, as we were outside in the open air. I soon discovered the reason for my feelings.

When we left in the morning, it was cloudy, although the clouds were way up high. As we continued to hike, the clouds appeared to be much lower than first thought. It's not like we were climbing Mount Everest. It was just that a fog was slowly settling in. They were so low that by the time we arrived at the Pinnacle, our goal, we felt like we were basically in a cloud. That was because, essentially, we were. We reached the platform and could see no more than a few metres in front of us. All I could do was laugh. Here we were, a German, a Brit and an Australian out in the wilderness, travelling a long distance from home just for the purpose of seeing the glorious view from this particular spot in the mountain range and we

The Other Side Of Travelling

couldn't see anything. It sounds like the set up of a lame dad joke. I have no clue what it looks like out there, apart from pictures on the internet. I hope to change that one day.

So we were unsuccessful in our initial goal. We decided to change tact. We had to tick something cool off of our bucket list. After travelling all that way, it was pointless to sit there being defeated. On the way down from the Pinnacle, it started to rain. So we had to do some research. After a bit of digging, we found some information that stated there were some relatively well-preserved cave paintings from the Aborigines. We set out and tried to check some of them out. We drove on a horrible, dusty gravel road for a good, long time. It felt like I was driving on corrugated iron. I am still impressed that my little green Toyota Corolla survived the drive. After what seemed like forever, we arrived at our first stop. We got out of our car to find the gate locked. There was a very small sign explaining that, due to the recent bushfires, the whole area was damaged. As a result, the cave was closed until such time that it could be restored.

We tried another location, same deal. Apparently, the whole area had been devastated recently by fires and they were still in the process of recovering. Eventually, we found one painting in another location about a twenty minute drive in the opposite direction from where we had started. It was found in a small cave, some distance away from our Cabin. Bunjil was the name of the figure painted.

Bunjil is somewhat like the creator of the world according to the Aboriginal people in the area (different tribes had different names and traditions). The painting was in a few different colours and Bunjil was drawn like a very large, round man. It was really interesting and had an eerie vibe to it. It seemed like as good a place as any for a creator to hang out.

We tried to visit as much as we could, including a decent Aboriginal cultural museum, but with all the rain, it was quite hard to get around.

Eventually, after failing to achieve most of our goals, we

Daniel Greenwood

had to head back towards civilisation. Of all the trips, this one was my most unlucky in terms of not doing what I had planned. Yet, waking up in the morning, opening up the blind and finding an emu staring back at me was an experience that I will never forget. It's nice to get out in nature every once in a while.

The Other Side Of Travelling

(The river where Kylie fell)

(A dead snake and cane toad, found by student)

Daniel Greenwood

(Lovely weather at the Grampians)

(Fish in the Great Barrier Reef)

The Other Side Of Travelling

(Demonstration Aboriginal Hut from Kuranda Tour)

(The friendly wombat at Healesville Sanctuary)

Daniel Greenwood

(Chain for support down Cradle Mountain Track)

(My clear view from Mount Wellington)

The Other Side Of Travelling

(View from AirWalk, Tasmania)

NEW ZEALAND

Happy Birthday

When I first got my passport, I wanted to try flying internationally. I didn't want to go too far, just in case it was not my thing, but I needed to experience something new, so I picked New Zealand. Really, it was the logical choice. It was only a four hour flight away from Melbourne, my home-town. So, if there were any problems, I could take the morning flight and be back in town by midday. I booked a five-day holiday to visit the North Island. I had very little specifically planned. This was simply testing the waters and nothing like my planned to the minute round the world adventure that I would go on a few years later. Most of the time was planned to be around the Auckland area, with one day trip planned for caving in the Waitomo Caves to see the glow worms there.

As I landed in New Zealand and went through customs for the first time, I had a feeling of excitement coursing through my veins. I hopped on the bus heading to the centre, and while on the way there, I had a discussion with a nice German lady. Her name was Franzi and she had short, brown hair. She was planning on WWOOFing (which stands for Willing Workers On Organic Farms, essentially working for food and board on a farm) for the next year or so. She had a male companion, Mark, that would be joining her. She gave me her number and organised a place to meet up that evening if we were both free. I was already enjoying the trip.

My first day there was a pretty simple affair. I got to the hostel (which, back then, was a first for me), dropped my pack

The Other Side Of Travelling

and got the feet moving around the city. While Auckland had a lot of the same stores as Australia, there felt like a difference in some key cultural aspects that made me sure I had done the right thing. I came home after the first day of travels and ate my quickly-cooked food in the hostel kitchen.

I soon got a text message from Franzi, saying that I should come to this bar near my hostel. Figuring, why not, I got dressed and headed out. I got there, shook hands and we got to chatting. It was all going well. Too well, in fact. It was then that I fell into the stupidest of traps ever.

Mark wanted to make a little bet with me. He said, "We will race. Whoever drinks the cider the slowest, has to buy the next round." It seemed fair. I agreed. We got our pints, and off we went. He managed to finish his in about four seconds.

That should have been the end, but unfortunately for me, I have a competitive streak. I somehow got it into my head that he just got lucky, and so gave it another shot. The German looked surprised, but was not going to say no to another free drink. So, we went again and I, of course, lost miserably. I paid up. I didn't want to play again. I had just learned a very expensive lesson. Generally speaking, someone doesn't propose a bet unless they think they can win. In a bar, no one proposes a bet unless they <u>know</u> they can win. Never, ever take a bar bet, unless you know the game they are playing.

I left soon after, and even kept in contact with Franzi. We would meet up sometime later when she came to visit Melbourne and introduced me to a bunch of cool people that helped me on my trip.

When I arrived back at the hostel, there was a Japanese man sitting by himself. I was not entirely sure of hostel etiquette, but I had read online that people often meet randomly in these establishments, so I went and sat down. The guy looked at me, seeming very confused at first.

I explained why I was there and asked, "Is it OK if I sit down with you to eat?" I wanted to hear about him and what brought him to New Zealand. He was very excited at the prospect and nodded his approval. After a few more spoonfuls of soup, he said, "I am here for a small holiday to celebrate my birthday." I asked, "Are you travelling with other people?" He explained that he was also travelling alone. I asked him when his birthday was, to which he replied, "Today."

Well, a guy celebrating his birthday alone just would not do. I went out immediately and bought a cheap bottle of vodka from the store on the corner of Queens Street and that of the hostel I was staying at. I came quickly back and explained why I had bought it. He was shocked, but seemed appreciative. I just realised my mistake as soon as he poured me a shot. I wanted to give it to him as a present. I don't normally drink and had not realised that he would want to drink with me. It was not my greatest moment of integration into normal human social conventions.

Regardless, I drank the shot and we proceeded to do our best to finish the bottle. About halfway through, we were both quite giggly. I decided that I needed some food to balance out the alcohol. In true stereotypical Aussie fashion, I took out some Vegemite. My new Japanese friend looked interested and asked if he could try it. For those of you that are unaware, Vegemite is a sticky, jet-black substance that sticks to the roof of your mouth when you eat it. It's extremely salty in taste. Most people hate it unless you were brought up on it. As a result, the recommended amount of Vegemite for beginners is about a sixteenth of a teaspoon. For most people, this is still too much. My Japanese friend was a bold man, so he took a tablespoon, dipped it in, and took about half a tablespoon of the shiny, black stuff into his mouth.

I guess he was expecting some kind of Nutella. The smile on his face slowly faded. His eyes told me that he had realised that it was not chocolate spread. He quickly removed the spoon from his mouth and struggled to swallow. Taking a glass of water, he drunk until the taste was gone. It took a while. I guess he didn't like it and he looked quite warily at it from that point on. Like it might jump and attack him at any moment.

Eventually, we finished the bottle, became quite sleepy, and went to our respective rooms. Before I left, though, he had a present for me. He made me an origami crane. It was a really small gesture, but very thoughtful. I still have it in a box somewhere – it's a cool memory.

Hungover on a boat

The next morning, I was once again reminded why it might not be a great idea to drink so much. I had planned to get up really early to take a ferry to Rangitoto island, hike up the mountain there and enjoy the view. This idea to me seemed like not the best idea anymore; I was queasy and feeling very under the weather. I walked down the hill from my hostel to the pier. I was a lot slower than I would normally have been. I had to take a few breathing breaks too, to stop breakfast from coming back up to say hello, yet I was determined and got on the ferry.

The water was extremely choppy, which did not exactly help the feelings in my stomach. As we hit each wave, I felt the insides of my stomach slop around. At some point, some people started to notice me going green in the face and hence invited me to sit with them. They even offered me some food. I gratefully accepted the seat but not the food. I think any food intake would not have stayed long inside. I don't think my saviours would have stayed long either.

Looking up at my heroes, I soon found out that they were two South American women, specifically from Brazil. One, whose name was Larissa, was lean and dark-skinned with long dark brown hair. The other, Juli, was very pale-skinned with black hair that was tied back into a ponytail. They were both in Auckland to learn English. I can only say that having wonderful people such as these two girls looking after me was not the worst thing in the world that could happen to me, given the circumstances. They were also heading to the mountain and we decided we should hike together. I discretely ditched the ticket for the fast ride up to the top, deeming it more interesting to walk with the girls than ride up with a bunch of random people.

Getting off the ferry, we took our time and made our way to the top. We took so much time and were so casual about it that we actually walked a good forty minutes in the wrong direction and ended up on a smaller hill. However, there were some farm animals there and we checked them out before heading back in the right direction.

It was relaxing to be out in nature and Larissa would sing songs all the way up. We all hit it off and by the top of the mountain, Juli, Larissa and I were already talking about meeting again. The view from the top of Rangitoto was amazing. There is a volcanic crater there that is worth seeing (much more impressive than Mount Edna) and a panoramic view of the bay area around Auckland. After we had had our fill of the beautiful view and had a snack, we made our way back down. We took the boat back together, just as the weather turned bad and it started to rain. At the pier, there was a gelato store, which they showed me and we sat down for a snack.

I met both of the girls the next day at the school where they were learning English. It was there that I met the other students in their group. We hung out for most of the rest of my stay. Most of the time, we visited the sorbet store at the pier, at the base of Queens Street. For some reason, Larissa and Juli seemed to have an obsession with coconut sorbet; I never saw them eat anything else. I wonder if that is the popular thing over there.

Anyway, by the end of my trip, I had a series of contacts that I would use on my travels around the world. I really could not have done a lot of the adventures that I did if it was not for those girls taking the chance and talking to me. The friends that I made through them echoed through my entire trip. The day after that, I headed towards the caves, which was the only planned part of my trip.

The Other Side Of Travelling

Are you sure that this is what the professionals use?

The caves of Waitomo are special because you can see a particular species of glow worm. You should look them up on the internet. Glow worms are not as cute as you might think. They use their glow as a lure to catch insects. However, it looks pretty cool when you are in a cave and you see all those lights above looking like stars. At Waitomo, you have a few options to see these organisms.

One way to get a glimpse of the glowing worms is by taking a small boat ride in an easily accessible cave, where a lake is situation within. Another is to ride on a large doughnut-shaped inflated rubber wheel that takes you gently down a river in the cave and allows you to soak in the visuals. I, however, was in for the adventure experience.

The day I woke up, it was raining. Hard. I got on the bus for my journey there. If I remember correctly, the whole ride was about two hours or more. About halfway there, I got a call from the company.

The tour group that I was with had cancelled the visit to the cave due to danger caused by the heavy rain. However, I was halfway to the location. The company had found another tour group that was going into a different cave and explained that this cave was less affected by the rain. In hindsight, I should have trusted the company that cancelled, but I was determined and so I agreed to join this other group.

I arrived about an hour later and was given a wet suit to put on. I was also given gumboots and a helmet. I remember thinking that these shoes are not exactly useful for climbing in caves. But, the excitement was such that I was still pumped with adrenaline and probably not thinking straight. The guides that were to take us through the cave were two very relaxed New Zealanders.

We took a car from the headquarters to the cave. On the drive there, once they found out that I was Australian, we swapped jokes about each others' countries. What I soon learned is that we essentially say the same things about each other. I won't go into detail here, but let me just say that a large portion of our jokes about one another involved farm animals.

We arrived a short time later and proceeded to the entrance of the cave. It was still raining. Rather heavily in fact. The entrance to the cave was narrow. We had to enter sideways, as it was too narrow for any other way. After continuing like this for some time, we eventually stopped. Water from outside was running past our feet off a thirty metre drop. There were ropes and other equipment. We would be abseiling down and continuing through the cave to find the glow worms.

They had briefly explained to us how to abseil back at the office, where we were given our gear and, after a short reminder, the first of the two instructors went down. Then the first person in the group followed. I was the third to go down.

Around ten metres into my attempt, I hate to admit that I was struggling. I didn't have the right technique and I was giving myself some pretty bad rope burn. However, I was unsure how to change and I didn't really want to test theories while up in the air. I had to proceed down as I was.

About halfway down, I heard the noise. I looked up and the flow of water from above had increased substantially. My height and position on the line meant that the water first hit me right on my upper chest and face. I felt like I couldn't breathe from the weight. I think I just got unlucky with the angle. I wiggled on the line, eventually managing to do a hundred-and-eighty-degree spin, but then the water was hitting my legs. The weight and momentum spun me around on the line. Spinning and spinning, I couldn't see, and was barely able to breathe. I had no choice. In my panicked state, I let myself down, fast and blind. It was not the smart thing to do, but I was not thinking clearly. I managed to brake about a meter from the ground. I then dropped into the pool of water at

The Other Side Of Travelling

the bottom. This was not the adventure I had planned or the smooth James Bond-esque entrance I had hoped for.

We continued on through the cave. I climbed, crawled, ducked, dodged and dived through. The water was about six degrees and I was freezing, despite the wetsuit. We went deeper and deeper until we finally got to a point where we could see the glow worms.

We turned off our headlamps and looked at the glow. It was beautiful – chemiluminescence at its finest. I wanted to sit there for a while and just admire the craziness that evolution had produced. However, as deep into the cave as we had gone, we had to come back out eventually. We couldn't climb back up the thirty metre drop. That meant climbing back out through a different path. This is also where those gumboots caused me problems. Major problems.

While admittedly, not feeling all that great about the trip, I tried to keep participating and getting all the best out of it. At one point, we had the option of the ladder or the rock face. I picked the rock face. As I was climbing up, water started to run down my chest and legs, running into my boots. The further I climbed, the more water there was in the boots. By the time I had reached the precipice, both boots were so full of water and my legs were already so tired from the climb that I couldn't get my leg up on to the ledge. I was stuck. I managed to wedge my chest into a small crack and my arms were up on the ledge, trying to give myself a rest. It didn't work though, and with every passing second, I became tired of holding myself up.

Eventually, one of the instructors had to climb up and help me take off my boot to get rid of the water. Then we were able to finally get me up onto the ledge. I was thankful for the help and felt a little embarrassed with my lack of sportiness.

When I left the cave, I was so tired that I barely remembered the worms. I do remember the bloody hands and legs and the aching body for the days afterwards. I would do something like this again, but I would suggest trusting the advice of the company when they say it might not be the best idea to go. Perhaps a little training at a rock climbing park might help too.

You can see me?

I got back to Auckland pretty late that night after the cave trip. I was super tired and kept falling asleep on the bus. A young Maori girl was singing quietly in the back of the bus. It was a nice sound and it helped me to relax and calm down after the big adventure. I am not as tough as I try to be.

When we arrived back at the bus station, I started walking my way back to the hostel. As I headed up the massive incline that is Queen Street, I saw a homeless man on the street. This is not an unusual thing. There seemed to be a large problem with homelessness when I arrived in Auckland. I hope it's better now. Regardless, he looked around forty years old. He was short, with short black hair that had some streaks of grey in the front. It looked like it had been cut recently, and he seemed to be looking after himself as best as he could. He was wearing jeans that he had cut into shorts and no shoes. As I passed him, I gave him some money, smiled and continued on my way up the hill. He got up instantly.

"You can see me?" He was so surprised. I assured him that I could. He began by explaining, "I have been invisible for a long time. You are the first person to see me in days." He asked if he could walk and talk with me for a while; I said that he could, of course. We talked a lot about small things, the weather and such. It wasn't exactly like we were reading the same books or had a lot in common, but it was not awkward either.

It was about halfway through our conversation that he said something to me that was extremely interesting. He stopped me, looked me dead in the eye and said, "I hate that the government says I'm gay just because I like to suck dick." I asked if he didn't like gay people. He replied, "I just don't like labels."

The Other Side Of Travelling

It was an interesting way to look at it. I suppose sometimes labels can be more harmful than useful. This is especially true when the labels don't fit what the person feels they really are. If they have been pigeon-holed into one thing, but perhaps take attributes from a number of categories, the labels can become oppressive. I was pondering all of this for a short time. It seemed that it was the end of his conversation. After that bombshell, he went on his way and found a new place to sit. I hope he doesn't have to stay invisible for too long this time.

The next day, after saying my goodbyes to Larissa, Juli and my other friends, I headed home. My thirst for travel was awakened.

Learning the hard way

About six months after my first visit to New Zealand, I took a second trip. I was bored in my job and was saving every penny for "the big trip". However, I just couldn't resist going back and hanging out. It was partly to visit the friends I had made on my previous visit. Many of them were still there and were still learning English. I was happy to catch them again.

Larissa, who you remember from my first trip, and Johnny, a Taiwanese gentlemen that Larissa had introduced me to on my last day, took me on various trips, including to a super cool beach called Piha with pitch black sand from volcanic ash. Larissa and Johnny, along with Peggy, who also went to the English school, also took me to a strawberry farm. I lost my camera card at the hostel, so I don't have many records of that time, but the photos I do have show amazing scenery.

But, even as I was in Auckland, the itch to see new things caught up with me. I decided to take a flight down to Christchurch to see South Island. I had heard of the amazing scenery that was there.

The flight was pretty easy and when I arrived, I found my hostel pretty quickly. Unfortunately, just before I had arrived, the first of a series of tragic earthquakes had taken place and the aftershocks were still to be felt while I was there. Every now and again, there would be a shaking of my bed, then it would go still. It was not necessarily scary, but a little eerie perhaps.

I met a Mexican man, by the name of Diego, in my room. He was a pretty chilled guy and was just checking out New Zealand while he waited for his Australian visa to go through. He was going to go live in Sydney with his girlfriend. He was a musician and he taught me a few cool tricks on the guitar.

One day, I offered to share my dinner with him. I was leaving the next day and I had cooked tacos using the remaining food I had in the kitchen. He gladly accepted. After an hour of cooking, I put the dish on the table. Diego looked up at me.

"What have you made?" He didn't look disgusted or anything, more just unsure of what was on his plate. I was confused. I explained that it was tacos. He took a second to register this and then laughed. He smiled at me, took a shell, filled it with the toppings, and took a bite. Then he nodded. "It tastes pretty close to tacos, but the shell is weird." I asked him what he meant, at which point I got an explanation that the hard shell tacos that Australians are familiar with don't really exist in Mexico. It's more of a "Tex-Mex" thing, apparently. "It tastes good though", he assured me, going back for seconds.

From that conversation, I learned an age-old lesson that goes something like this. All food that is labelled as exotic has probably been altered dramatically to suit the new market. If you think Thai food is hot in Australia, try it in Thailand. You don't know tacos until you have been to Mexico. You haven't had Bolognese until you have eaten it in Italy. That is not to say that the varieties back home are bad – they taste nice. Still, they are not the things that they are labelled as. No, they are some kind of hybrid.

I am awesomeness personified. Just don't check my pants.

I wanted to visit some of the more scenic areas of the South Island of New Zealand, so I took a bus tour to Mt Cook. It was a long drive there. On the way, as I stared out of the window at the landscape, the first thing I noticed aside from the beauty, was the lack of houses. Anywhere. It was then that I was told that the whole south island had something like one million residences. That is crazy. If this was Europe, then it would be so densely packed that you could barely breathe. I'm glad that it is not covered with houses though. It meant that there were lots of wide open spaces, which was great to see. We haven't destroyed all of the beautiful places yet; we are still trying though.

There were many things to see along the way. My favourite and most memorable sights were the lakes. The particular shade of blue that the lakes had was the weirdest and most unique I had ever seen. The guide tried to explain that it had something to do with a chemical that is eroded into the water by the glaciers. It gives it this amazing colour that you would only believe is photoshopped unless you saw it for yourself. I never got around to checking the science behind it, but it is on my list.

But the best thing was yet to come. As we rounded a particular bend in the road, we finally saw our goal. Mt Cook. It was as epic as one could possibly imagine. We stopped at a convenient location near a small church where you could see a large section of the mountain range. Clouds were rolling over part of it and it just didn't look real. The lake at the base of the range seemed to go on forever and had that same amazing blue colour. There was an opportunity to take a helicopter ride from a nearby station and land on one of the glaciers. I was plenty afraid of heights, but an opportunity like this does not come often, so I took it. It would be my first time on a helicopter.

I got into the helicopter and immediately freaked out. As they started up the motor, I could feel the whole door move back and forth against my left arm in time with the rotors. The two people next to me were smiling and taking photos. The pilot put on his headphones and adjusted the throttle. I could feel the engine working hard against a little thing called gravity. The rotors sped up. The air was being forced down and around us. Eventually, all the forces aligned and we were off.

With my heart racing and my wallet hurting from the expense of the ticket, I was not sure what was more scary – hurtling through the air in this little metal box with sharp metal blades or seeing how casually the pilot was driving the helicopter. From what I could see, it looked like he was steering with one finger. Every gust of wind hit the helicopter and pushed it slightly off-course. Despite this, the pilot was unfazed, casually chatting to us. We got to the top, landed, and I tried my best to be as cool as James Bond would be in a situation like this.

I stepped out of the helicopter, put on some terribly unfashionable sunglasses, and walked on the snow, acting like I did it every day. My heart was racing and I felt like throwing up from the flight, but I think I managed to hide that pretty well. I did feel a little like a bad-ass and totally forgot about almost messing my pants. I was on land again and feeling great. I looked out to the mountains opposite and the clouds were still rolling over. It was amazing. I got a photo of myself with the help of the pilot, looking as casual as possible and then, just as quick as it had come, it went away again.

We made our descent and through the front window I could see the lake with its amazing blue water. However, the wind had picked up and was bashing our helicopter around. The pilot was still loosely holding the stick as he explained that we would be the last tour for the day, as it was too dangerous to fly out again. The weather was too crazy. I didn't understand how he could say that and not grip the stick a little more

The Other Side Of Travelling

securely. I was holding on as tight as I could. Not that it would have helped much if something went wrong.

Eventually we landed safely and I got back in the bus and made my way back to Christchurch. In the end, it was an eight hour journey, with one hour of intensity and seven hours on the bus looking at the scenery. It was a long day, and a tiring day, but totally worth it. I flew back from there the next day to Auckland and spent a few more days enjoying the company of my friends Larissa, Peggy and Johnny, eating gelati at the ice cream store at the pier. Larissa still got coconut gelati. It must really be a thing. I then flew back to Australia, returning to reality for a second time.

Daniel Greenwood

(Lion Rock, Piha Beach)

(Boat ride towards Rangitoto)

The Other Side Of Travelling

(View from Rangitoto Peak)

(View from Ben Ohau Mountain Range)

Daniel Greenwood

(Helicopter ride back to ground level)

(Queen Street, Auckland)

BRAZIL

Delays

Eventually, about two years after my initial trip to New Zealand, I had worked up the courage to do my big, round the world trip. I had been saving all the cash I could, occasionally bleeding a bit of it for short trips back to New Zealand, but finally, I had enough to do what I wanted to do. I decided to leave from Melbourne and move east. In this manner, I would eventually fly around the whole world and arrive back at home; it was a neat idea.

The first destination on my list was Brazil. I planned to spend a few days in Rio and then go visit my friends in Belo Horizonte. I had two friends there, having met one on my first trip to New Zealand, Vinnie, and one on my second, Juliana. Both were very cool and promised to look after me when I arrived in their home town.

I planned my trip meticulously. I had a massive Word document on my computer with lists of sites I wanted to visit and things I needed to do, places I would stay and rough costs to keep me on budget. I had booked all the hostels, paid for as many of the events as I could, and just made sure everything was going to be awesome. I wanted to get as far as I could with the cash that I had, so I had to know where the money would go. I didn't want any nasty last-minute surprises cutting my holiday short because I was out of cash.

Eventually, after what seemed like a lifetime of waiting, the big day finally arrived. I was dropped off by my mother. I thought she would cry and was prepared for all of that, but in the end, she was pretty smooth about it all. She understood why I was going and wished me luck. There were a few tears from her and my sister, but I think they did alright.

Waving goodbye, I started my battle through the Australian customs. It was an annoying process to go through, but I didn't let it bother me. I was off, this was it, my big trip. Adrenaline was pumping. I went through the duty-free, I had a look at all the specials and decided that the hype was not worth it. So, I didn't get anything. After a casual, calm stroll, I arrived at my gate. It said on my ticket that boarding would start at around 9 am. I had arrived at around 8:30 in the morning. It would seem that there was a plane delay and it would not leave until 1 pm. This was not the start I had in mind.

I was tired, having not slept well the night before due to excitement/anxiety. Trying to maintain my optimism, while struggling considering the thought of the fifty hour flight that was ahead of me and the delay not making it any shorter. When 1 pm came, I finally got on the plane.

The first leg was a flight from Melbourne to L.A. I would have a seven hour overlay there and then fly to Houston. A quick flight change would take me to Rio. The plane ride was not bad. However, being unable to sleep, I watched many movies. They had a self-service fridge at the back with drinks and chocolates which helped keep the energy levels up. I arrived in L.A and was walking a little zombie-like and perhaps slightly manic looking, through the customs. I was contemplating just how far away I was from home, when I was stopped.

"Excuse me, Sir, can you step aside please?" Of course, I complied. With how tired I was, you could have told me anything and I probably would have done it/believed it. They explained that they were doing a random check and wanted to ask a few questions. They asked me, "Why are you coming to America?" I explained that I was flying to Brazil. Officer Two asked, "Why are you flying to Brazil?" I explained that I was visiting friends. They both wanted the names of my friends

The Other Side Of Travelling

and a lot of other details. They didn't write it down, I think they were just trying to trip me up and get me to hesitate. Eventually, my story seemed to suffice and I was allowed to continue. After clearing customs, I spent much of my seven hours at McDonald's. It tasted almost the same as at home, but the Coca Cola cups were much bigger. I had asked for a small. The cashier told me it didn't exist.

I got in line to go through the X-ray machine for the flight to Houston. On my way through, I was asked some more questions by TSA about why I was there. I explained and then got on my plane. It seems something about my look made me very popular with the security teams in L.A. Or perhaps, that is how they are with everyone.

It was a short flight to Houston. I had no problem there; the people were nice and guided me in my almost catatonic state with gentle announcements to my plane. A long time later and after more sleepless travel, I arrived in Rio.

By this stage, I had been travelling for more than fifty hours, and by my own estimation, I had been awake for about forty five hours of it. I was out of it. I had spoken to a guy in the seat nearby while on the plane. We had a pleasant conversation. He was an American, working in Rio. After a while, I guess he decided that he liked me (or pitied me) and he offered for me to come with him to the beach in the taxi his company was paying for him to use. I accepted.

If I was tired, I found out very quickly that a taxi ride in Rio is the instant wake up. Four cups of coffee could not have had the same effect. He was flooring it through traffic. I am still surprised to this day that I made it there alive. He would often look back at us to ask questions while he drove. While I was thankful for the interest, I fear that my answers may have been a little short.

I had a Cola with the gentleman who paid for the cab at a small kiosk on Copacabana beach. Eventually, my new friend had to go and I made my way to the hotel room my mother had paid for as a gift. She had done it so that I had a nice place to sleep when I first arrived. It was clean, had a fridge, and was close to fast food. I was very thankful to have a private room. I could sleep without interruption. It was one of the better presents my mother has given me. I went out for more McDonalds. Not the best of diets, but the jet-lag was horrible and any kind of food was welcome. I think I passed out around 6 pm and woke up at 5 am. Not a bad nap. Also, not a bad time to wake up if you want to take advantage of the day.

James Bond is shorter than I remember him

I decided that I had to keep moving to fight the jet-lag, so I dragged myself out of bed. I got a map at the kiosk and forced myself to walk to a place called Sugar Loaf Mountain. A taxi would have been much quicker, however, I would have fallen asleep on the way. I would have to do it all on foot. As I walked through the streets, I really began to get a picture of just how big Rio actually is. My feet were almost bloody stumps by the time I reached the mountain.

There is a cable-car to the top of Sugar Loaf. I hate heights (I might have mentioned that once or twice at this point) but figured it was the best thing to do if I wanted to get a good overview and some nice surroundings. Also, as far as I could see, there was no other way up and I was not walking back now without seeing something cool. I remember that when I got on the cable-car, the weather was not so inviting, a little cloudy. However, to my luck, it cleared right up by the time I reached the top.

I would be lying if I said I remember all too much from Sugar Loaf Mountain. It was all a jet-lagged blur. Also, for most of the cable car ride, I was not looking out, due to the whole "afraid of heights" thing. There was one thing though that I could have remembered even if I hadn't slept for a week. While walking around the boundary fence at the top, with my glazed over eyes staring at the beautiful scenery, I heard a high-pitched squeaking noise.

Looking around for the source and checking that I hadn't stepped on a cat or something, I struggled to find where it was coming from. After some time of fruitless searching, I finally found a small monkey. It was a kind of small marmoset, black fur with tinges of red and white and a fluffy tail. It looked kind of like it had sideburns. To be perfectly honest, with the way the hair was arranged, it would seem I had found the inspiration for the early hairstyle of Hugh Jackman's Wolverine. Still, it wasn't quite as intimidating on a little animal like that.

I stood still. It looked at me. I looked at it. The monkey decided I was not interesting and continued on its mission. I was curious what it was doing. Something about its behaviour seemed suspicious. All of a sudden, its whole posture changed. It was low to the ground, crawling near a kiosk. In my head, the theme from Mission Impossible was playing. It entered the kiosk from the back door and then there was a screech – it was discovered. The monkey ran off and parked itself somewhere near the kiosk. I guess it was waiting for the next opportunity.

Sadly, I don't think it got one. Tourists heard the commotion, saw the cute little monkey, and started gathering around while taking lots of photos. But they gave it food. Perhaps its skills were lacking because it didn't need to practice anymore.

My selfie is better than yours

I eventually made my way down Sugar Loaf and headed from the mountain to the most iconic of tourist destinations in Rio, the famous Christ the Redeemer statue. It was an eleven kilometre walk. My feet were hurting already, yet, I was determined. I walked and walked and walked. By going on foot, I got to see all sides of Rio. I went through both the rich district and the poor district.

Everywhere I went, people looked at me. I realised that they all thought I was stupid. It was midday and the sun was insanely strong. Everyone else was under the shade, sipping from coconuts while I was pounding the pavement. After another half an hour, I agreed that I had made a bad mistake and found some water and a place to take shelter.

After the break, I continued and finally arrived at the base of the mountain where the statue is built. It was a half hour wait for the train up to the top. The chance to sit down and a nice cushy ride up was far too appealing after the massive walk I had done, so I waited and took the easy road. Don't judge me.

Once I was on the top, I had another three hundred and sixty panoramic glimpse of the city. It was such an amazing sight. Most other people were taking photos with the statue. I looked at them with frustration. It was a clear sign of the fall of society. How could they be wasting such a vision with all their ignorant selfies? Did they not see all the wonderful sights around them? Also, I'm very, very short. How the hell am I supposed to take my selfie with all of them around? They would be ruining my shot.

At the end of the day, I was jealous. All those tall people could take their photo without all the other posing tourists. They could then post it to Facegrams or Instabooks and pretend like they were the only person there. I improvised and managed to get my shot looking like I was alone and convincing myself that mine was necessary, unlike all those other people's, as I made my way back down. I did manage to push my way through the crowd to have a look at the surroundings from the top. It was gorgeous. You could see the beaches, the city, the trees. There were so many vibrant colours; it screamed "life".

I started heading back to my hotel. It was a long way away. With about three kilometres to go, I have to admit, I almost cried. I was tired, hungry, and sore. I had a travel card and tried to take some cash out for a cab, but my card only worked in certain ATMs and I couldn't find one that would accept it. I would be walking the rest of the way. I finally arrived at my hotel and then basically passed out. Jet-lag had overcome me and I didn't wake up until 10 am the next day.

Eventually, I dragged myself out of bed and I walked around more of the beach area. There are workout stations all along the beach, although they were mostly designed for body weight exercises. The equipment was brightly coloured and the places were always full of people. It was amazing to see, not only were the perfectly sculpted males and females working out, but the grannies and the guys with beer guts were keeping active too. It seems to be something which is built into the culture.

The other thing that was definitely built into the culture is small swimwear. For everyone. Regardless of age, shape or size, there was not much fabric. To be honest, I started to question why they even bothered. They might as well have been naked. However, it was an interesting aspect to see all the same. I got to get a good understanding of the human form in all its beauty. I could not quite bring myself to partake in the culture though; I didn't feeling like bringing out a g-string. Maybe after a small workout?

I should have gone to see more of Rio, and I hope to go back there one day, getting more in touch with the culture and perhaps visiting some museums. But, at this point, I was too damn tired. I really hoped that I would be able to change that as I moved forward.

Fight for Your Right to Party

After Rio, I flew to Belo Horizonte, where I met up with two of my friends, Juliana and Vinnie, that I had met in New Zealand. The first half of my time there, Vinnie let me stay with him and showed me around. He was so welcoming and introduced me to all of his family. They made me feel like I was at home. It is a tough town there, but there is a cool music scene.

At one point, Vinnie took me to a bar where a band was playing on the side-walk. It was there that I saw my first real confrontation with the police and the people of Brazil.

The band was playing at the request of the bar and it seemed like the bar had some kind of permit to let this happen. The band was jamming and everyone was having a good time. I was having an absolute blast and just enjoying the company of those around me. Vinnie had introduced me to the band and we were dancing, enjoying cheap drinks and meeting new people.

All of a sudden, out of nowhere, two policemen in their greenish uniforms and SMGs had decided that the party was stopping, permit or no permit. One officer did most of the talking, while the other aggressively gripped the gun slung over his shoulder. There were heated discussions from both sides but eventually, the police let it go. I had tried to understand what was being said. Sadly, it was all spoken too quickly. My Portuguese was not up to scratch for such things. However, I did talk to the people afterwards and they explained to me that, unfortunately, in Brazil, this is a normal occurrence.

It seemed to be nothing more than a reminder of the power of the police over the people. This is a theme I heard much about during my time in Brazil. The people and the government were clearly not happy with one another and it could be felt and seen through all the interactions. It seemed that something big was building and neither side could or would back down. Brazil was on the edge of something big.

It was not the only place that I saw such things. There were heavy police forces everywhere, either in green or in blue uniforms. One was national and one was local. Either way, they were visible, visibly armed, and not particularly happy-looking people. I am not sure if I felt safer by seeing the guns or not. It was a curious effect. I don't want to put a damper on Brazil; it is a great place and you all should go if you get the chance. However, at the same time, there are some things there that need to change.

Food, Glorious Food

After a while, as I spent more and more time in Belo Horizonte, I came to notice something – McDonald's was rather popular. It tended to be popular wherever I went, but here was different. It was almost like a status symbol. The food cost the same as it would in Australia. However, with the average Brazilian wage being far less than that earned in Australia, McDonald's actually works out to be way more expensive. That would be like paying fifteen to twenty dollars just for the burger back home.

I wanted to understand why people were still buying food there…it just didn't make sense. They could buy fast food for a quarter of the price that was the same quality, but just didn't have the McDonald's name. So, I looked at the crowd entering. They were all rich. Whereas in Australia and America, McDonald's is often a refuge for the low socio-economic elements of the population, in Brazil, it was for the rich. To spend money like that on crappy food showed just how much money you had. It was as I said before, a status symbol. It's interesting how dynamics change in different cultures. Food is an important part of Brazilian culture.

For the whole second half of my time there, I stayed with Juliana. She was a cool chick, studying law, and she spoke quite a few languages. Smart girl. She was very accommodating and started by taking me out for food. Her restaurant of choice was Outback's. I wasn't sure if that was a joke or not. Having just left Australia, "Outback's" was the least-expected option available. The toilets even had "Sheila" and "Bloke" on them, really embracing the inner Crocodile Dundee.

After lunch, Juliana and I went to the movies to see "Paranormal Activity 4." I must admit, it was a pretty scary movie. However, I did not get any frights and I did not scream, because no matter how scary the content on the screen was, the people in the crowd were so funny. I couldn't keep the frightening atmosphere in my head. They were screaming, laughing, yelling at the screen, talking to one another, and food was flying. It seems like going to the movies in Brazil is more of an interactive experience than it is in Australia. I walked out of there laughing. It is the little experiences like that, that make the trip worth it.

We then went back to her place to meet the family. Juliana's mum didn't speak a single word of English. I spoke enough Portuguese and when we didn't understand, we used Google translate. However, there was one way of communication that always worked.

The language she spoke to me was food. I guess Juliana's mum had decided that I was too skinny. When I left my room, she was there with food. When I left the house, she would not let me pass without shoving food into my bag. When I got home, she would give me food. There would be food there on my bed or a snack while watching TV. There was enough food for about three of me. I guess I was supposed to eat it all. I did what I could and it was very generous of her, but man, I would have been about one hundred kilograms heavier if I had managed it all. I got a good workout though from carrying all the extra weight in the backpack.

Also, later on in my trip, as I was starting to run low on funds, I thought back to those moments and thanked her, because if I had bought all my food then, I likely would have been starving later. No matter how much you plan, you are going to go over budget somewhere. Juliana and her family saved my butt.

Something is wrong

Over the course of my short time in Brazil, I made lots of other friends. Everyone was so generous. One night, shortly before I was to head off to San Francisco, I was invited to a party by the band that had been playing at the bar. Vinnie was going to be there and I went along too.

The Other Side Of Travelling

I was immediately welcomed by everyone. I had so much fun. They even tried to get me to play guitar, but when I tried a lame version of "Freebird" at ten times the normal speed, they gently took the guitar back and gave me a drink instead. There was a neat kid there, the son of a girl named Amanda, that I got along with (though I think he saw me as a moving Jungle Gym). Amanda had bought a bottle of vodka for me to share with her. I drank what I could and then eventually the party slowed down and we all went to sleep. I slept in the backyard, on a bench. The weather was warm enough that I didn't even need a blanket.

When I woke up, I was feeling a little under the weather. Amanda's kid had found me and wanted to play games. I did what I could for a while, trying the old tricks like pulling a coin out of the ear and throwing him up in the air. However, with every minute, it became harder and harder to concentrate. My hands were tingling and I was feeling queasy. My eyes even felt slightly blurry. I was in trouble. At first, I thought I must have had a hangover. But, I had not had much to drink, and no hangover causes the symptoms that I had.

I turned to Amanda and asked her to take me to a doctor. This is when I learned that the medical system in Brazil is messed up. She took one look at me, laughed and said something to the effect of, "you are not dying, they would not even bother to see you." However, she did see the seriousness of the situation and so with the help of one of her friends, they managed to get me into a car and drove me somewhere.

I say somewhere, because at this point I was really struggling to follow what was going on. Eventually, after about twenty minutes, the car stopped, they got me out and took me to an apartment. I don't remember what it looked like. It seemed that it was the mum of Amanda's friend and she was a nurse. She took a quick look at me, gave me some medicine, and then they put me to bed.

When I woke up (I am not sure how long I slept), the kid's face was about ten centimetres from mine. I think he was watching me to make sure I was OK. He was a good little dude. He ran and got his mum, who came to see me. I was feeling a little better. I managed to get myself out of bed and they drove me back to where I was staying. I slept most of that night and half of the next day. When I finally got up out of bed again, I was fine.

I don't know what the hell happened, whether it was something I ate or if I was bitten by a mosquito. I don't know what medicine I was given or how long I passed out after that. However, I do know one thing – if I had been staying in a hostel, I would likely not have received help anywhere near as quickly as I did. I was lucky that those people took me in and cared for me. Even if it would have gotten better on its own, the panic of feeling like that in a place where I was barely able to speak the language would have been terrifying. They helped me to keep calm. I'll never forget it.

Eventually, after an amazing time there, it was time to fly back to the USA. I was very sad to say goodbye to all my new friends. It would be my first real lesson of life on the road; you meet so many wonderful people and then never see them again. You have to learn to enjoy the time you have with them, make a good memory, and be glad you got the chance to meet cool people. Take the lessons of your time together and carry that with you. If you are super lucky, you meet some of them again. But if not, you had a moment of awesomeness and that is something worth cherishing. I would eventually get used to moving on to the next town, but, saying goodbye would never get easy. It would always be a mixture of excitement and sadness.

The Other Side Of Travelling

(Kiosk after crazy taxi ride, Copacabana)

(The cable car, Sugarloaf Mountain)

Daniel Greenwood

(James Bond, Monkey Secret Service)

(Christ the Redeemer, Rio)

The Other Side Of Travelling

(View of Rio from Christ the Redeemer, Rio)

(View of Belo Horizonte, Brazil)

USA

Déjà vu

My plan was to fly from Belo Horizonte to Rio, Rio to Houston, then on to San Francisco, then LA and finally San Diego. The flight to Rio was easy as was the flight to Houston but the flight to San Francisco would be broken up by an overlay in LA. I don't know why either. It just was. After many hours of flying, I got off the plane for the change to San Francisco. As a side note, if you have noticed, I had the worst Travel Agent ever, and from about this moment on, just booked everything myself. Going through to the next terminal, it was there that I was stopped. It felt slightly like déjà vu. Unlike last time, I had slept a little, so that helped with my recall.

They asked me, "Why are you coming to America?" I explained that I had friends in San Francisco that I was going to go visit. Again, they wanted to know, "How did you meet these friends?" I explained to the new TSA agent that I had met them in New Zealand. They wanted to know my full story, again. I had a suspicion the first time that my long beard and tanned skin had something to do with my popularity with TSA. After the third time I was stopped, whatever made me attractive to them was starting to annoy me. I started to get the feeling that LA was not ready to welcome me.

I got to San Francisco and just wanted to go to the hostel to sleep. Although it's not as long as the fifty hour flight from Melbourne to Rio, Rio to San Francisco is no short trip. However, the airline lost my baggage. So I waited for a few hours, found a power point to plug my laptop in, and wrote a few emails. They finally found it on the plane that was scheduled to fly to San Francisco after mine. I guess it got mixed up.

Free Riding

It was early November of 2012 when I finally landed in San Francisco. I was visiting friends there. Just like the majority of people I mention in the first half of my book, I first met Mimi and Shelby in New Zealand, while they were on some kind of exchange program. Unlike a lot of the others, I had met the girls randomly at a bar. We had kept in touch since.

When I first met Shelby, she had super long dreadlocks going on. She was a very sporty looking girl and seemed very relaxed at all times. By the time I got to San Francisco, she had cut her locks off and was wearing what I think they call a "pixie" hairstyle. I barely recognised her at first, but it didn't take me long to get used to the new look. Mimi was slightly shorter than Shelby and had some really cool bright red hair. Her style was a little less hippie-ish, although she was equally relaxed.

The first part of my time in San Francisco was spent with Shelby and Mimi showing me around the city and its surroundings. Shelby's boyfriend John came along too. He was a quiet dude with short black hair and a big smile. Super friendly. They even took me to Muir Wood forest. It was such a memorable location with gigantic trees. The age of the trees is mind-boggling. Sitting in the forest and thinking of all the things throughout the world that had happened while the trees continued to grow and gain mass was a humbling experience.

Eventually, the girls dragged me away from all the plants to head back to the city. At one point, after crossing over the Golden Gate, on the way back from the forest, we went for a drive towards the beach. We were on our way to Pier 39 so I could see a small seal lion population that lived there. The drive back gave me a different look at nature than I ever would have expected in a busy town like San Fran.

I thought I had seen skin while in Brazil, but I was about to find out the real meaning of freedom. I was looking out the window, still fascinated (read terrified) by the fact that I was driving on the opposite side to that of the Australians when I saw a shirtless guy on a bike. I could only see him from the waist up, as there were parked cars on the side strip where he was riding along.

I can distinctly remember thinking that it was probably a bit too cold in November for shirtless bike riding, even in California. Nevertheless, my trip was all about learning to deal with different people and cultures, so I wrote it off as something that just happens there. Besides, he really seemed to be enjoying the bike ride. He was smiling and nodding at everyone. A friendly dude.

Eventually, there was a gap in the cars. That is when I got my first glimpse of his penis. He was on my right side, heading in the same direction as us. Every time his left leg pushed down on the pedal, his right leg would raise. This would change the balance of everything and the penis would do a wide arc in the air before slapping onto his left thigh. Due to the shock of the sight before me, it seemed that there was almost an added slow motion effect. At that moment, I felt that, if I had a calculator, I probably could have worked out the parabola. I am sorry to describe it in so much detail. However, the details are burned into my brain. If I have to suffer, so do you.

So anyway, left leg down, right leg up. Well of course, the bicycle is called that because of the whole cycling thing. There was cycling to that movement too. So without fail, his left leg raised, his right leg dropped, and the penis went on a whole new arc. Again and again, back and forth, back and forth. I didn't want to see it, yet I couldn't look away. Have fun trying to sleep tonight, while getting that image out of your head. As I said, we are all in this together now.

I guess what was more off-putting than anything else was the fact that he had a helmet on his head. The big head I mean. The small head was totally enjoying the breeze running through its hair. I guess the guy was thinking of safety first, I suppose. I am not sure that the helmet would do much to protect his other exposed aspects from the elements if something was to go wrong. I guess he had the right idea to prioritise the top brain, but still.

I never found out if that was a normal occurrence as I was not there long enough. The only indication that I had of the normalcy of the act was the fact that people didn't seem to be that shocked as he passed them. Perhaps they were just averting their eyes...or repressing memories. Still, if it was a normal act in that fair city, someone should sell them reflective paint to keep them highly visible. Somehow, I feel that they would not have that much trouble sticking out in a crowd.

Mimi, Shelby and John were no help here either. I was so dumbstruck when I saw it, that I couldn't speak. By the time I could get my words out, we were well past the scene of the crime.

Riot

After all the excitement of the forest and the naked man, as well as a few more tourist stops including the Chinatown, I went to bed in the afternoon for a small nap. Mimi and Shelby went back to their place for a nap too. The city was quiet and I fell easily into a deep sleep. It had already been an eventful trip and I had a long way to go. When I woke up though, things were very much in a different state than I had left them.

Hearing commotion outside my hostel, I quickly put my clothes on to check out what was going on. Lots of drunk people on the streets was the first thing I saw. Interested to see the reasoning for the heavy partying at such a weird hour, I followed. However, eventually, by following the noise I found a whole group of people hanging out. Thinking it was a sort of festival or even a block party, I stuck around. I thought that it might get interesting. Asking one of the fellow observers what it was all about, they explained that the Giants (a baseball team) had won the World Series (a competition between mostly American teams) and that they were celebrating the victory.

I've seen a lot of celebrations in my short life. I have partaken in lots of celebrations. Believe it or not, I have even initiated some celebrations. The crowd was more than celebrating. Things were on fire. I don't mean cakes or anything. I am talking rubbish bins. Street lamps were being swung on. Street signs were being hung from and then broken. To this very day, I still don't understand it, but as far as I can tell, they were celebrating their city winning a major sporting event by trashing it. I have heard of riots taking place when a team loses or when rival fans clash in the streets. Yet, for me, for the winning team's fans to smash up the home-town is a mystery.

As the night progressed, things were getting heated, both because of the fire and also because the group was growing bigger every time I looked. Having seen enough popular TV and movies on jail life in America, I decided to take a step back. However, I was still curious and keen to see how it was going to develop. I am an interested observer after all.

Bus windows were smashed, more fires were lit, cars were jumped on like they were trampolines and dented. It was crazy. There seemed to be some rioters that were trying to direct traffic. Even in such drunken chaos, a few were trying to get some kind of order to their destruction. You could see the battle of their conscience. They would point away from the crowd, directing the car to drive down an empty street. Some of the other rioters would see the car, starting to run and jump on it. There would be hesitation and then finally, the Good Samaritan would join in on the Audi trampoline session. It was an example of mob mentality at its finest.

Obviously, this couldn't be allowed to continue indefinitely, so the riot police came. They were decked out in full armour and obviously not to be messed with. The majority of the rioters were too drunk to even notice the police at first.

The Other Side Of Travelling

Eventually, they worked out what was going on and lined up against the dark blue uniformed officers.

This is when things got bad. There was a second, smaller but more determined riot group, that must have been wandering the city. They soon found the group that I had been observing and met up with them. Now the riot police were in the middle of two angry/happy drunk groups of people. They started throwing bottles at the police. However, the police did not react. Before long, I understood why. At first, I thought it was their iron will to resist. But no, it was simpler than that. The idiots were each unaware that there was a rioting group of people behind the police. All the bottles were flying over the police line and hitting their fellow drunk citizens on the other side. The more one side threw, the more that came back in response. Each side thought they were giving it to "the man", but they were just giving it to each other. I must say that they probably deserved it.

After I heard more sirens and another ten police cars arrive, I knew it was time to go. I did not want to get caught up with the police at this time. I was not the only one on the move. Throughout the riot, a number of entrepreneurial-type people had been selling fake Giants t-shirts in the middle of a riot. They seemed to be making good cash, although they scattered as soon as the ten new cop cars arrived. I headed back to the hostel, shaking my head. At least they seemed to have fun.

I caught Shelby and Mimi one more time before I left that crazy city. We went out to a Halloween party. Don't ask me where because I don't remember. All I do remember is that the girls were very insistent on me drinking cranberry and vodka. I had never had it before. It tasted OK. Mimi had put a bunch of make-up on my face and we had gone to the party as zombies. Shelby had sugar skull make-up on and both of them looked pretty impressive. John was a centurion. I was very happy with my zombie outfit too. I had picked up a shirt from a thrift store and put a bunch of fake blood on there. I had never done Halloween before and it was nice to do something like that with a bunch of friends.

I do have some vague memory of them taking me and trying to teach me how to dance. I am terrible with dancing and I will always remember their patience and support as I flailed around the dance floor. What can I say? I just have no rhythm for that kind of stuff.

But, as I said, cranberry and vodka. So, no more info than that. I do remember waking up on a couch though, so I think the girls got me back to a friend's place. Man, am so glad I don't drink often. Party life is not for me.

A License to Chill

While talking about California, I might as well discuss my time in Los Angeles. I hit L.A straight after my trip to San Francisco. Yes, as always, I was stopped by TSA when I arrived. It seemed at this point to be a little ritual almost. I definitely factored the TSA questions into my estimated time spent in the airport.

My hostel was located in Venice Beach. As soon as I was out of the airport, I took a shuttle bus straight to the iconic beach-front. All I knew from Venice Beach was what I had seen in GTA Vice City. So, not much and quite a lot at the same time. The main reason I was in LA, was to take a tour of Sony Studios and to check out the La Brea Tar Pits, where they had found a bunch of mammoth bones. Totally exciting right?

I checked into the hostel and wanted to go straight to see the fossils. Sadly, it was too late in the day for that. I would never have made it in time. So, considering I could see it from my window, I decided to check out Venice Beach first.

It was a pretty unique location. It was loud, with lots of skaters, people covered in tattoos, and a lot of weed. While I walked down the street running along the beach, I heard a weird mix of music. As I moved just out of the range of one set of speakers, the next would come blazing in. If I stood right at the edge of where each stereo could reach I would get these

The Other Side Of Travelling

amazing mash-ups of the two songs being played simultaneously.

One thing I also noticed was that there were stores dedicated to helping people obtain their medical marijuana license. In fact, there are places in Venice Beach and all throughout the city where you could get such a thing, if you wished. I had even heard that it was relatively easy to obtain one, so I decided to check it out and test the hypothesis. I had no belief that I would get anywhere with it, nor would I have any real use for it if I got it. However, I was curious about the process nonetheless.

As I approached the establishment, I could hear the man outside screaming at people as they passed, reminding them that they could get their medical marijuana licenses there through them.

For example, at one point I heard him say "Get your licenses here, ladies and gentleman. We have doctors ready and waiting to help you with your needs."

I decided to talk to this consultant. The man was a giant. He must have almost been two meters tall and was built like a tank. His uniform hung loosely over his body. He could have squashed me in about two seconds flat. It was a little intimidating, especially considering that he was still yelling as I approached.

I'm still not quite sure what effect the words being yelled at me were supposed to have, but I guess he was using this technique for a reason. If it was me, I would be playing some John Lennon and talking very softly to everyone, trying not to kill their buzz.

Anyway, after I approached, I walked up and in my best, "I'm definitely doing this for legitimate reasons" voice said, "one medical marijuana licence please." Very quickly the consultant turned from a screaming promoter into a very astute businessman. It was as if Mr. Hyde had turned back into Dr. Jekyll.

He even started using legalese on me. "Before we begin, I

need to ask. Are you a resident of California?"

As soon as I heard that question, I was so bummed out. I was clearly a failure. I didn't even make it past the first stage. I was so boy scout that I couldn't even get a legal marijuana license which I would never use. I politely replied no, bowed my head in shame, and thanked him for his time.

He stopped me at the door. "Wait, wait, wait", he said in his subtle, smooth negotiation voice "Are you sleeping here tonight?"

I said, "Sure, I'm staying a hostel not far from here." As soon as I said that, his eyes lit up and he explained that, "Under the current laws of California, while you are staying in California, you are technically a resident for the purposes of the license." So clearly, I could have one so long as I was in the state, but it would expire when I left or could no longer prove my residence.

The next question he asked was why I needed it. I had not got that far ahead in my planning, thinking I would surely not even get past the first stage of the inquiry. I had to improvise. So, I said the first thing that came to my mind. "I can't sleep." This was true. Between all the long haul flights and nights in hostels, sleep was something I couldn't even remember anymore.

Again, the gentleman smiled. "Excellent, insomnia is one of the conditions on the list that qualifies for help."

If I had to guess, I would say that insomnia is a common problem in California that only weed can fix.

It was at that point that he explained, "Before we could continue, you would, of course, need to see a professional doctor to verify everything."

They clearly didn't just give these licenses out with a lollipop and a bag of weed; they had to be for legitimate medical reasons. The freebies came after. Given that I was in L.A for only a few days and that, regardless, I wouldn't actually smoke the weed, it seemed like a waste of time. I had many other things to do. So, I declined, figuring the time spent was not worth the reward.

Despite this, he was still ready for me. Like a business ninja, he had an answer for everything. He explained that, "We have a doctor working in a building not far from here and that they would see you in twenty minutes if you like."

That was a time-frame I could get behind. I wish I only had to wait twenty minutes for my legitimate health problems. Excited about the continuation of this interesting procedure, I agreed and we moved to the next stage.

I filled out a standard-looking medical form and waited in line. It took a long time and I was not sure why. I kept checking my watch and as the twenty minutes came and went, I was starting to get bored. The people around me seemed to be not at all bothered by the extensive wait times. As I continued to wait, I started to analyse the people around me. Some looked like they might have a genuine need for this license, while others looked like they were in the exact same situation as me.

At around forty minutes, the wait was too long. I wanted to leave. However, just as I was about to get up, my name got called and so I entered the doctor's office. It took me a while to see if the doctor was actually in there. There was so much smoke in the room. Finally, enough of the haze cleared and I was able to greet my doctor.

An old man, about sixty, big thick-rimmed glasses, with a comb-over greeted me. The hairstyle seemed to be actually for stylistic purposes, as he was not bald. He also had a lab coat on. A stethoscope hung around his neck. He looked professional...enough. I thought it would be quick.

He looked over my form. It seemed to be going well, although he appeared to be moving almost in slow motion. About halfway down the page, he saw my profession. As soon as he read that I was a teacher, his eyes widened.

"What an honourable profession", he exclaimed. "One of those jobs that should be paid more and respected more."

I nodded in agreement, and was glad for his appreciation

of my profession. However, I was hoping to leave soon and hoped that this wouldn't take too long. It did though and the next twenty five minutes were spent with him talking about how amazing the teaching profession is and why they should be paid more. He also talked a lot about how, "These kids are addicted to the Facegrams or the Instabooks or whatever these things are." That was the gist of it, anyway. To be honest, there was a lot of points when I had no clue what he was talking about. I started to suspect he might have been testing the medicine before administration.

He didn't even stop rambling about teaching as he did the check-up. I had a jacket on. He took the stethoscope and placed on my left arm over the jacket. For those of you that don't know what it does, you can basically hear the heartbeat or issues with the lungs. Which means that it needs to be placed on the chest or back. It is absolutely no use on the arm. I know people talk about wearing your heart on your sleeve, but this is taking it too far. Not that it seemed to matter. He was nodding like he could hear something, with a big smile on his face.

Clocking in at thirty five minutes, after eventually getting around to asking about my sleeping issues, which I again did not lie about, he finally gave me approval for the license.

"I just need to sign this and then you can get registered." Taking out a pen from his front pocket, he made the motion of signing the document and handed it to me. His eyes slowly looked up at the door, as he clearly was trying to get ready for his next customer.

Upon looking at it, I realised that he hadn't actually clicked the pen down. I am still not sure how someone could make such a rudimentary error. If I had to guess, it was likely that either he must have got a hit from the bong for every patient he passed or he was five months away from retirement and didn't really care anymore. I leaned over slowly, so as not to startle him, clicked the pen and politely asked for the signature again.

I had to hang out another ten minutes in the waiting room. The reason wasn't clearly explained. Finally, another staff member came and I was taken with my document, along with three other confused looking patients, to another dodgy looking building a good ten minutes walk from the main office where the license was registered.

After one more long wait, I was now able, if I was so inclined, to partake in the medicinal properties of the green plant favoured by Tenacious D. I did not choose to, however, with the drug itself being of no interest to me. The experience itself was way more exciting. At thirty USD for the license, it was the most expensive bookmark I ever had though.

I did take my shiny certificate and instead headed off to Hollywood Boulevard in search of the famous sign and other relics of the movie world. Still, I'll always remember that doctor.

Snoop Doggy Dogg

I took the bus up to Hollywood Boulevard. That in and of itself was an experience. L.A. really needs a train system; the bus system is too confusing.

Anyway, Hollywood Boulevard was just like I imagined. Dirty, smelly, full of questionable people in different furry costumes. Some of the outfits looked like they had not been washed in some time. All of them wanted to take photos with you for a small fee. I almost considered paying them to go away.

As soon as I arrived and got past the crowd of furry Disney characters, I found the stars of the important people (Chuck Norris and Arnold Schwarzenegger). I took a photo of the Hollywood sign. I went to Ripley's Believe It or Not. Interestingly, I did not believe most of it, but I was glad that they gave me the choice. Then I was done.

I was pretty annoyed, to be honest. The place is so hyped up, but at the end of the day, you are looking at stars on a

Daniel Greenwood

boardwalk. You are not meeting the person who belongs to the star; you are staring at a name etched into the ground, probably with some chewing gum or dog shit on it. Glamorous, it was not.

So, frustrated with the time wasted, I was walking back to the bus, listening to my music (Machine Head, for anyone interested), when a man stopped me. He had a big smile on his face. He had typical clothes that might be seen in any gangster rap video. Some sort of blue jersey if I recall correctly that was way too big for him. He said "Hello", so I said "Hello" back. He asked, "Where are you from?" I replied, "Australia." He asked for my name, and without thinking, I said, "I'm Daniel." That was a mistake. I had engaged too much. I was now in for the long haul. Whatever he wanted to say to me, I was now going to have to listen.

He began by explaining that he was an emerging rapper and that he had actually been signed to Snoop Dogg's record label. He showed me a photo on a phone I was not even aware was able to show photos. It must have shown a maximum of sixteen pixels of information on the screen. I could see that there were two people with dark skin in the image, but beyond that, who they were and whether one was Snoop Dogg or the other the man in front of me, was difficult to tell.

My new friend was happy and very sure that he had convinced me using his very solid evidence. He proceeded to write my name on a disc and sign it. It was a burnt disc with no label or other information. While I was contemplating whether it was "street" to have this style (look at me with my lingo skills) and whether Snoop Doggy Dogg would allow someone on his label to be out on the street like that, my new friend gave me the disc.

He kindly asked for ten dollars to help support a local artist (him). When I said that I didn't want it and that rap was not even my style of music, he explained, "Your name is already on it, who else would I give it to? It would go to waste." I explained that Daniel was not exactly a rare name, but out of good will, I would give him a dollar if he really thought he could not get rid of it. I didn't really believe that there was even music burned on there, but it would be a funny memento of the experience regardless.

He was not happy and started to complain. "I can't do it for that price." So, I walked away. Eventually, he chased after me and gave me the disc for the dollar. He looked at me as if I had hurt the feelings of an old friend. I think he was still hoping I would give him more cash. I walked off with my interesting purchase.

There was music on there, it was not bad. But, with my rap skills not being exactly A+, it could be that the music was illegally downloaded and not even his own. I never got around to really research it too much. If it was him, he has talent and should get somewhere in the music business. However, seeing that there were another twelve people around him showing the same pixillated photo and CDs, I feel that some of the music might have been borrowed from other artists.

The rest of my time in L.A was nice enough. The La Brea tar pits were epic and I saw my first squirrel there, but I have to say that when it was time for me to go to San Diego, I was glad to get out of there.

The Godfather is shorter than I remembered him

I flew out from LA (more random questions) and got to San Diego. My next flight in about five days was scheduled to leave from San Diego to New York. This time, it would be direct. I was glad to bypass LAX.

The hostel I stayed at was one of the weirdest I have ever been to. It had a clean kitchen. The rooms, on the other hand, were not of the best quality. The combination of people that were staying there was interesting, to say the least. They all had very "unique" personalities and back stories – no stereotypes here.

The people in the room I was staying in were using it as

a base to sell pot. One guy had got a big inheritance from his grandfather and was using it to stay at the hostel and record an album of some indie folk music. He was a little like Jekyll and Hyde. In the morning, he would wake up, go to the studio with purpose and motivation. When he returned, he would be extremely high. The companion of this musician/pot seller was tall and chubby, with short black hair and a pudgy face. They were friendly enough to me, and they were quiet after 1 am, so I was at least able to get some sleep. Still, they weren't the only unique people in the hostel.

There was another girl who I saw in the kitchen every day. She was really short. Coming from me, that is saying something. It was reasonably warm, about twenty five degrees. She had her hoodie up all the time and spent a lot of time laughing to herself as she walked around the place. I figured she was listening to podcasts, but I just couldn't see her headphones. Or maybe she was a little crazy and needed a place to crash. Better here than out on the street.

My first night, at about 2 am, I discovered that the music man and the crazy lady were connected. It seems they had previously been in a relationship. The guy had paid for a private room for the two of them by using part of his inheritance. They had a falling out and he had moved out into a dorm room. He explained to me, "I paid for a private room for a while longer to give her a chance to find something."

As I said, at 2 am, there was a knock on the door. It was the girl from the kitchen. She was screaming at the top of her lungs "Give me my wallet back." I looked to the music man and asked, "What is all that about?" He was very high at this point and explained that she had given him a wallet for his birthday. He pulled it out and showed me. It was a neat wallet. She wanted the gift back, and she wanted it now.

Eventually, the noise got so much that he couldn't ignore it anymore – he went to the door and in a very calm manner said something to the effect of "Hey". The girl was immediately silent. He took a deep breath in and was looking as if it was difficult for him to put all his words together into a sentence. He had smoked a lot of pot. Finally, after what felt like aeons, he managed to say "this is not the right time to talk, let's discuss this in the morning, OK?" She finally calmed down and agreed to have the discussion the next morning.

The next morning though, he was out of there like a flash by about 6 am. The lady came back and he wasn't around anymore. I could already see where this was going to go. I went around San Diego, checking out the few sights that were interesting to me and then headed back to the hostel for food. Some people were watching movies in the common room, so I chilled out there for a while. Eventually, I went to bed.

Around the same time that night, she came back screaming. Slow movements were all he was able to make. He had smoked way too much weed. I almost pictured him as a long-haired sloth, slowly moving through the room. He opened the door and talked with the screaming girl for about half an hour. If the conversation had been sped up to a normal pace, the talk could probably have been done in about five minutes, but he needed a lot of processing time.

The next night, when it happened again, I didn't wake up. After a certain amount of time, if you are constantly sleeping in hostels, anything becomes normal and you sleep through it all. However, while I slept through the banging, something else woke me up. I received a tap on my shoulder. He had woken me. My sloth-man friend sighed and said "Hey man", followed by another sigh. Being used to his low processing power at this time of night, and unaware of any way of speeding it up, all I could do was patiently wait. He looked so sad and bummed out. I sat there staring at him, continuing to wait for the reason he had woken me up.

Finally, the movements in his brain picked up enough for him to explain why. "I just can't handle it today man. She keeps killing my buzz. It's just too intense." He asked me to get rid of her. I explained that I could make such a thing happen, and wanted to know if he meant only for tonight or forever?

He replied that he didn't want to see her. He couldn't deal with the craziness anymore.

What I did next, I am not exactly proud of. Yet, I was tired and pissed off at the recurring visits. I do what I can to keep a level head. However, just like everyone, I too have my limits. In situations like these, when I am not exactly calm, the result is not often something that I am happy with or proud of later. The guy saying that he wanted her gone was the final straw. In my tired, frustrated brain, I pictured a traffic light changing from red to green. I had permission to let it all out. I got up and opened the door. I only had underwear on. All my terrible tattoos were showing. The whole time, the chick had been banging and screaming. When the door opened, she was expecting the musical sloth. She got something else instead.

I ripped the door open and screamed: "WHAT THE FUCK DO YOU WANT?" You could see the fear and confusion on her face. I was not the calm man she was expecting. I was not the calm voice she was hoping for. She took a step back. She managed to whimper, "I want my wallet."

I yelled back, "I DON'T HAVE YOUR FUCKING WALLET." You could see her recovering from the initial blow and getting ready for a counter attack. She clenched her fists and her whole face was going red in anger. I had to do something to cut her off before she started to let loose on me too. "FUCK OFF AND NEVER COME BACK HERE, OK?" and I slammed the door in her face.

When I looked back at the guy in the room, he had his mouth wide open. His eyes were wide too. I don't know what else he was tripping on, but it took a long time for him to say anything. He just stared. Eventually, the cogs started moving and he said, "Dude….you are the Godfather." I went back to sleep. I wasn't even sure if he would remember what happened when he woke up or if he thought it was all a hallucination. However, I hoped that it would be the end of my involvement in this soap opera.

The next morning in the kitchen, I walked in with my

head resting on my chest. I was still so tired and just wanted a cup of tea and some food. Music man (in fully awake mode) and his friend were there already. Spotting me from across the room, he yelled at the top of his lungs "GODFATHER." I looked around me. Was the movie playing on a screen somewhere? What the hell was he referring to? He pointed at me and screamed it out again: "GODFATHER!" He beckoned me to join him. It seems that he was referring to me.

He told the story to his friend. As he was not high yet, it did not take too long. In fact, he was quite articulate in his speech. His friend turned to me and said, "Dude...you ARE the Godfather."

This was becoming surreal. I really hoped it wouldn't catch on, but after this, everywhere in the hostel I went, these two guys would yell "GODFATHER" at me and cheer. They didn't explain to anyone else why I was being called this and it resulted in a number of very weird and interested looks.

Learn the rules

On one of my final nights in San Diego, I went to a bar with a fellow Australian. We would be meeting a girl named Teresa later that night. Teresa was a very tall lady with dark brown hair and brown eyes. She worked for Intel, doing something super complex and impressive that I couldn't quite follow. I think it had something to do with analytics. Either way, she seemed like an intriguing person to hang out with. However, we had time to kill before that, so my fellow Aussie and I decided to go and chill out at a bar, called "The Shout House", near the hostel.

We left relatively early, so we got a spot and found out that we had arrived just in time for a dual piano performance. Sure enough, at the other end of the room, two pianos were placed, facing each other. Curious as to what the hell a dual piano performance was, I was excited to stay and check it out. My friend agreed and we moved closer to the stage.

In my head, it was going be some epic piano dual, like a drum battle, but with pianos. It was not quite that, but it was still cool. They played some music and then started taking requests. One after another, they played a bunch of songs. My friend and I also put a request into the hat.

About an hour into the performance, they read our request out. It was "I Come From the Land Down Under" by Men at Work. The two players looked pissed off. Finally, they spoke into the microphone. "It seems that we have a request without the customary green paper there. The song is a good choice though, so we will play it." With that, they were off, singing the song that all Australians know.

It took us a second to realise our mistake. We had not tipped the musicians, when we put the request in. Suddenly, I felt so embarrassed. I had turned into the dumb, uninformed tourist that I so despised. I had simply assumed they were paid by the bar to keep people there and buying drinks. But it was more like busking in a bar. We each got some cash out and dropped it into the bucket out front. Having redeemed ourselves, we were able to relax again.

Still, it was an important lesson to learn. It is almost impossible to avoid making mistakes like that wherever you go. When you do, just be graceful, say sorry, correct the wrong thing when possible, and burn the rule into your mind so that you never make the mistake again.

After the performance, we met Teresa at another bar nearby and had some fun listening to some horrible '90s music. I am not a good dancer, so I didn't stay long. I had originally pictured Teresa to be a total computer nerd, but as soon as she hit the dance floor, the girl was off and swinging to the music. I was impressed and a bit intimidated at her skills. I have never been comfortable in clubs. I am just too self-conscious with this sort of thing. I said bye to Teresa and the Australian fellow and was on my way. I could still see Teresa burning up the dance floor as I left.

I left the bar, went home to the hostel, and tried to get

some sleep before my flight to New York the next day. I had a gut feeling it would not go so well; there had been storms and hurricanes in the NY area, and the news kept talking about all the problems in New York City. There was also a new storm front coming in. I was hoping just to get to New York before it all went to shit.

Don't bother running

Back at the hostel, I fell straight to sleep, but I was woken up by screaming at about 4 am. This time, instead of at our door, it was coming from outside. I got up and looked out through the window. A guy was running, while holding onto a bicycle. He looked like he was afraid of something. He kept running and screaming but I couldn't see what he was running from.

I soon got my answer, as a cop car drove up behind him. The lights were on, but there was no siren. He was driving behind the guy running away. Eventually, the cop must have had enough, drove up onto the footpath, got out of his car and grabbed the screaming guy. The guy was yelling out the whole time "WHAT DID I DO? WHAT DID I DO?" as he was being dragged into the police car.

As far as I can tell, there was no explanation given. In the back the guy went, and off the car went, hopefully back to the station or hospital or whatever it was that the guy needed. It was one last, timely reminder that the rules are different in each land and that when you are in someone else's country, make sure you follow the rules. You do not want to be going to jail for a stupid mistake.

Sliding planes and expensive taxis

I finally finished my time in San Diego. It was only five days, but it felt like a whole lot more. The time came to pack my bag and say goodbye to the room-mates in my hostel. It would be the last time I was called "the Godfather" on the trip.

I went to the airport to take my flight to New York. Shortly after arriving there, as I tried to check in, I was told that due to the recent hurricane, flooding, and snow storm that happened in November of 2012, I would have to fly back to LAX and then take a plane from there.

It was like time stopped. My head span. Not LAX again. Any airport but there. Send me to Washington, Florida, San Francisco, anywhere, but don't send me back to LAX. They hate me there.

Not to disappoint, upon arrival I was selected for a few "random" questions. "Why are you in LAX?" I explained that I didn't want to be there. "Where did you want to be?" they asked. "New York", I calmly responded. "Why do you want to fly to New York?" Rather than continue to transcribe a repetitive conversation, for more instances of my questioning in LAX, check out my stories from Brazil. It will give you the same picture of what I went through now. It continued until eventually I got out of it and caught my flight to New York.

I was flying towards Newark Airport. If I haven't mentioned it before, I hate flying. I really hate it. The whole way there, it was a little bumpy. As we flew closer to Newark, the turbulence became worse. But what didn't help me to alleviate the fear was the landing on the tarmac. It was snowing and this was the last flight before the airport was closed due to the snow storm. The plane slid a little bit as it hit the snow-covered tarmac; I nearly filled my pants.

Grabbing my bag from the checked luggage and getting out of the airport, the situation was not much better. Due to the disaster, there was a city-wide shortage of gasoline. Buses were not running. I would have to take a taxi if I didn't want to stay the night at the airport. Due to the gasoline shortages, the prices were jacked up. A taxi from Newark to Manhattan was going to be at least four hundred USD. Luckily I managed to find three other people to split the cab with me. This helped me out immensely. It still hurt my wallet, right in the money part, though.

When I arrived at my hostel, after paying the gentleman driver, the only place that I could get to in order to buy food was a small convenience store near the hostel in Queens. From a wide selection of junk food, I got myself some Frosties Flakes and sat down to eat them at 11 pm at night. It was not the most nutritious meal, but better than nothing under the circumstances.

A guy from Germany with long blonde dreadlocks and a funny little goatee/moustache combination saw me and introduced himself. His name was Ollie and he asked me, "Are you enjoying your three-course meal?" He invited me to hang out with him. I had nothing else to do, as going outside into the snow storm was not an option, so hang out we did. I would eventually meet up with him again in Berlin for some more shenanigans.

The beds in the hostel were very clean. In fact, they were almost too clean. This discovery was made as I lay down to sleep my first night there. It was then that I heard it. A sound like I had sat on a plastic bag echoed through the room. It was a little like if you take a plastic bag and swish it between your hands – not necessarily loud, but a penetrating and distinctive sound, nevertheless.

It would seem, that in an effort to combat the overall disgustingness that people in hostels tend to leave, they had lined the pillow and mattress with some sort of plastic. This kept the whole bed clean and the mattress and pillow themselves were not uncomfortable. However, every time I moved, breathed or thought, the plastic moved, waking myself and those around me. I never thought I would have to deal with a situation where the problem was a hostel that was too clean, but there are always firsts. I'd still pick that over the damp, filthy hostels of Darwin.

Never meet your idol

In all the stress and craziness that New York was going

through, trying to get things back online and the massive city running again, I missed a spoken word show by Henry Rollins. I was quite disappointed, as I had booked this before I even left Australia. If you haven't heard of the guy, it is definitely a worthwhile evening. He has lots of cool stories and he's one of my inspirations for travel in the first place.

Anyway, I was so bummed out, but I remembered that there was another show the next night. I called up and explained the situation. The establishment ("Joe's" I believe it was called) was helpful and said that, while they couldn't guarantee a place, I should show up and they would see what they could do to make something happen.

I arrived at the show, a little nervous that they may not have found anything. I stated my name. The lady at the front didn't even need to look up anything. It seems she was aware of my predicament and had a solution. I was led behind a door, upstairs, where I finally ended up in the sound box. These are seats normally reserved for guests, so I was extremely lucky to be there.

The show itself was great. The stories were awesome, although it did make me feel guilty that I had not included Africa on my trip. He made it sound so amazing there. I will get there one day. I managed to meet the guy after the show and he was really cool. He actually even smiled. I didn't even know he was capable of doing that. I got him to sign my ticket, chatted a little and asked for a photograph. I wanted evidence.

Up until this point, he was about five millimetres away from my face. It seemed like he was trying to absorb every single word that I said. It was a little intense. I looked at his smile and decided that it might just be a grimace as he put all the information from me and the other people into his brain. When I asked for a photo with him, he turned, put his arm around me and immediately the face turned to a look of anger. I suppose he has a reputation to uphold.

When I look back at the photo, I look like a man who cannot believe he has met his idol. Interestingly, that does not make one look good. I look like I lost at least thirty IQ points as I stare in an "I can't believe its happening" sort of way. One of the cooler moments in my life has been recorded, and I look like an absolute idiot. That's how it goes. More often than we think.

I met lots of other cool people and made a lot of friend at the hostel. I did a day trip to Philadelphia and went to an interesting medical museum there. I also saw the Liberty Bell. It was a bit over-hyped.

Back in NY, I also got to check out a show from David Letterman. They caked so much make-up on his face. Roughly every five minutes, as they took commercial breaks, he was being covered with half a kilogram of new make-up. I wasn't sure how he was able to keep his head up by the end of it.

By about halfway through my time in New York, they had fixed the subway after the flooding from the hurricane. That made movement easier. I visited Brooklyn Bridge, Central Park, the Natural History Museum and many other iconic sites. The Statue of Liberty was closed, but we did take a ferry that past it on the way to Staten Island, to get a closer look.

After about twelve days in New York, around the middle of November, I made my way to the airport to fly to Dublin via Frankfurt and London. If I haven't told you already, I had the worst travel agent ever. Book things yourself. Seriously.

Daniel Greenwood

(From San Francisco Riot, 29th Oct 2012)

The Other Side Of Travelling

(Just before I saw the guy on the bicycle, San Fran)

Daniel Greenwood

(Sea Lions, Pier 39)

(Street Art, Venice Beach)

The Other Side Of Travelling

(La Brea Tar Pits)

(My first squirrel, Los Angeles)

IRELAND AND NORTH IRELAND

Wallace

Dublin was not the town I had expected it to be. Years of exposure to typical "Irish culture" on the television did not prepare me for the reality. Dublin is a tough town, with plenty of character. There are lots of nice people though, and lots to do. I first went to Dublin Castle. It was to be the first castle I would see in real life. In my head, I had pictured a draw bridge, moat with alligators and maybe some soldiers with bows and arrows pointing at me, as I humbly ask for entrance to the magnificent fortress.

I was pretty tired after the long flight from New York, but was trying to stay up and fight the jet-lag. So, I was hoping for something really exciting to keep me energised. I must admit, when I got there, I was a little disappointed and let down. The castle did not bring the ye' olde feel. It looked more like a government building of a paranoid prime minister who built a wall around it. Regardless, while aesthetically appealing, the experience was underwhelming. Failing at the castle front, I decided to tick off the next typically Irish thing I could find.

I dragged my tired, sore body to the Guinness Brewery. This was a strange choice for me. I cannot drink Guinness. When I come into contact with gluten, my body attacks itself. So, no gluten for me. However, let the record note, I was on the gluten free diet, before it was cool.

The Other Side Of Travelling

But the museum looked relatively interesting, so I went and checked it out. Even if you can't drink the stuff, the process of making it is fascinating and Guinness seems to be a drink that divides people. You either drink it or you don't. I have heard many an argument at bars over that drink.

As I went through the museum, one of the coolest parts was that, included in the price of entry, is a drink. The drink itself had absolutely no interest for me. I couldn't drink it, but it looked nice. The reason why I was excited was that you could take a class to learn how to pour a Guinness properly. The process is not one for someone who wants their drink now. It is a very elaborate pour process, with mathematical angles needing to be applied to the cup for optimum pourage and a specific wait time while the drink sits and rests before you can top it up. So, while not being able to drink it, the experience did give me the chance to picture what it would have been like to be a bar tender in a local pub, where everyone knows your name.

I did go to a few more sites in Dublin, and even went on a bar crawl. However, ultimately, while an interesting city, there was not much in it for me. A lot of it is modernised and my heart lies in the ancient world. So I looked around for something more to my particular taste.

I found it in a town called Trim. There is a castle there and it was creatively called Trim Castle. An American girl, around twenty five with dyed black hair, named Jennifer, as well as a thirty year old New Zealand guy, tall and lanky, called Nick, who carried around an expensive camera, came along with me for the journey. The lens was as big as his forearm.

This is where I give an example of why it can be good to travel in the off season. Jennifer, Nick and I arrived and were the only people there. The guide explained that there was meant to be some other people coming who were on a bus tour. For some reason, they had been delayed. He was bored and tired of waiting for them. So he started the tour just for us.

The place was empty besides us. However, while the guide

was explaining details about the construction of the castle, I couldn't concentrate too much on the whole tour thing because there was something distracting me. The guide was carrying a giant sword around with him. He seemed very casual about the whole thing. He was using it to point out things of interest and such. A little too much swinging for my liking.

At the end, he explained that he carried the sword because a part of Braveheart was filmed there. Now, don't get confused readers. Braveheart is a movie about a Scottish man, played by an American who some claim is Australian, filmed in an Irish Castle. To make it worse, the scene the castle was used for, was for the siege of York, an English town. The legitimacy of the Hollywood industry is clearly shown.

The guy let me hold the sword and I got an epic photo with the light glinting off the sword, me holding it up in the air, striking my most terrifying pose. I looked thoroughly unintimidating. Nick took the shot. You know you're cool when even a giant sword can't make you look slightly scary.

A discussion and a meal

The next day I moved off to Belfast to see all the cool things there. I took the train from Dublin and found a seat with a table so I could put my laptop up and get some work done. A lovely elderly couple sat opposite me.

After a while, we got to talking. They were curious about what I was doing. I started talking about my goal, explained where I had been and told them some of my more interesting experiences so far. They were keenly interested and kept asking questions. It helped to pass the time. Eventually, a food car passed. I looked into my wallet, hoping to find a few coins for a chocolate bar or something. I was not going to be able to afford it. The elderly lady I had been talking to must have seen me, because she bought me a bunch of food. When I said that I couldn't pay her, she explained that I had paid for it with my stories and gained a lot.

Of course, I'm not sure how much they actually enjoyed my stories. However, I was thankful for the food. Every time I start to worry about humanity, something like that happens. It was such a kind gesture and one that I try to pay forward when I see others in a situation like I was. I know I keep saying this, yet it is true. I would not have made it anywhere as far as I got without the help from all these people along the way. I have been very lucky.

I arrived in Belfast, where I took a black cab tour to see how the troubles went and hear stories from someone who had lived through some of the harder times Belfast has seen. My driver's name was Paddy. Over the course of the tour, he told us many of his life experiences and losses during the troubles. It was an amazing and difficult experience to process and I recommend that everyone take a trip in there to hear the real stories from the locals. You don't get that many opportunities like that.

I also went on a tour to the Giants Causeway with a tall, red-headed, bearded Australian named Richie (we are everywhere, aren't we?) and a German girl named Sarah, working for Google in Dublin as a translator. She was short and wore her blonde hair in a ponytail. We saw many things, and even went on a famous suspension bridge. I did not like the heights. I do admit though, it was cool, once you got across the unstable, swinging bridge made of chains and an unstable footpath.

After I was done with those awesome trips, I went back to Dublin for a few more days. There, I met some lovely people at the hostel that made my time there much more enjoyable. Every evening, I had dinner with up to fifteen other people in the common room. It was like having a giant family. After being so long alone on the road, it really made my day. In particular, I remember a guy named Toni, who was from Spain. There was also a Brazilian girl from Sao Paulo, named Marcelle. Finally, a Mexican lady by the name of Maria rounded out the core group. We went to see one of those James Bond films when they came out. We also hung out at a local bar, which was lots of fun. So, thanks to those three lovely people and all the others I met there. It really made a difference and their friendliness stayed a strong memory for the rest of my trip.

On my last day, I said my final goodbyes to my hostel family and then, I flew on to Scotland. I'd like to just drive the point home of how crappy my travel agent was. My flight was from Dublin to London Heathrow, where I had to then switch airports to Gatwick and take a flight from there to Glasgow. At Gatwick, they even confiscated my Vegemite. Bastards. While the flight itself might have been cheaper, the cost of the transfers between airports and other expenses meant that I would have paid double the cost of a direct flight there. I really hate that guy.

The Other Side Of Travelling

(Trim Castle, Ireland)

(Dublin Castle)

(Street Art, Belfast)

(View of coastline in North Ireland)

SCOTLAND

You certainly keep odd hours

I finally arrived in Glasgow to find that, on top of all the other time wasting on flight transfers, British Airways had also lost my bags.

So, when I finally got to the hostel in Glasgow, I was sour to say the least. I checked in, made my way up the elevator and got to my room. Before I even unlocked the door, I could hear the snoring. I was tired and pissed. However, you can't complain to the guy for something that was out of his control. For two hours, I tried to sleep, but it was just too loud. I was too angry to sleep anyway.

At about 3 am, he finally stopped snoring. I got excited. I thought "Finally, I would get a few hours shut-eye." However, this was not to happen. This gentleman woke up, got down from the bunk above me, turned the light on and started studying. Patience is something I normally have. But not that night. I stood up, and punched the light switch off. Then I just glared at him for a while. I had bent the switch into the wall. I lay down.

The next morning, the guy wouldn't look at me. As the sun poured into the room, I got a survey of my surroundings. Ramen Noodle packets were everywhere. The room stank. I didn't need a light to work that part out. From what I could gather, he was living in there semi permanently.

After about two days, I decided to go to Edinburgh for a while and hoped that when I came back, that there would be a different room for me available. I just couldn't handle it there.

Which was a shame really, as there was lots of cool music stores to check out.

Destiny was not so clear

So, after making the decision to get the hell out of there, two days later, I took the train out as soon as I got out of bed and arrived in Edinburgh before 12 pm. The very first thing I did was go to the Elephant House café. I had been listening to the audiobooks of Harry Potter all along my trip. By coincidence, when I arrived, I had almost finished the last book in the series.

The Elephant House café is where JK Rowling supposedly wrote the first books. So, I sat there, listening to them as I had an English Breakfast tea. I tried to imagine her in this café, writing, not famous, unable to imagine how many lives she would soon impact. I could see the castle through the window, which must have surely been the inspiration for Hogwarts. I finished the book just as I finished my tea. It was a nice example of good timing. If you go into the toilet, there is graffiti everywhere with notes of thanks to her. It is all a bit odd when you consider that I was in the gentleman's toilet. I doubt that she would venture in there to communicate with her fans.

Afterwards, I dropped my bag off at the hostel and walked around. The city is nice, but very hilly. It was sometimes tough walking up and down the streets and navigation was an interesting experience. Still, I got to the places where I wanted to go.

The next day, I woke up early again. As I came into the kitchen, I bumped into a guy named Christopher. He had been staying in the same hostel as me, back in Dublin. We had had a quiet drink in "The Brazen Heads". What a coincidence! He was a sharply dressed man from Canada, with a well-trimmed beard. I was impressed by how he managed to do that. By this stage in my trip, I looked like a cross between Frodo and Gimli.

The Other Side Of Travelling

I just hadn't had any time to maintain any kind of civilised appearance.

When I left Dublin, Christopher was still making up his mind as to what he wanted to do, so I had no clue where he was headed. Seeing him in Edinburgh just a few days later was a very nice surprise. I would catch him again, briefly, while staying in a hostel in London. So, let this be a reminder to you all. Be nice to people, because they do appear again, and again, and again.

We both left together and went out to do the Edinburgh walking tour. There were many highlights to see as Christopher and I walked through the narrow, hilly, curved streets. The guide, a big bearded man by the name of Alan, was taking us around the city and was mainly working as a comedian. He said, "I'm doing this tour in my downtime." He told many stories, but the story of the Stone of Destiny had to be my favourite.

The stone is believed to be the coronation throne for the old Scottish kings. If the story, as it was told to me is true, it was stolen by an English King and placed under the chair at Westminster Abbey, where most of the English monarchs were crowned. Eventually, in 1950, four students decided to take the stone back for Scotland, so they broke into the Abbey around Christmas.

They found the chair and removed the ancient stone throne. Removing the stone involved damaging the centuries-old English coronation seat. Then, they proceeded to lift the stone. They immediately dropped and broke it.

Just think about that for a second. You are going to be in a lot of trouble if you are caught, but the reward, in your eyes, is the return of the ancient throne to Scotland. So you go and rescue it. Then, you break it. Your status as heroes of the North are, at this point, questionable at best. One of the guys took the smaller bit, got into the car and said "Good enough." The others used a jacket to slide the larger piece into the other car.

They were nearly caught by a policeman and fearing they

would be caught at the border, they stashed the rocks away to hide the evidence until the situation cooled down. The larger part was buried, with the smaller part left in the car at a friend's place.

They eventually got the stone pieces to Glasgow, got them fixed, and placed them in an Abbey. The priest saw the stone and probably freaked the hell out. He knew what the stone was and didn't want to be charged for stealing it. By 1952, it was back under the chair. The participants put in all the effort with the only result being that the stone was now broken and back where it started.

In the 1990s, the Prime Minister returned the stone to Scotland on the condition that it came back for the Coronation of the next Royal. With how tough Queen Elizabeth the Second is, I'm not sure that day will ever come. You can find the stone at Edinburgh castle. I did check it out and it was pretty cool.

After my tour finished, I went up to the castle. The outside that I had seen was great and very castle-like. The rest of Edinburgh castle was quite interesting as well. It has a huge history and lots of important events happened there throughout the years of its existence. As I walked around, I was looking over the wall that gives a view of the big park below and saw something strange.

Way, way down in the base of the valley, there was a bunch of people dressed as Santa Clauses. There must have been at least a hundred Santas there. Then, they started to run around a track. It was a Santa race. I have no clue why, but it was an interesting spectacle to see nonetheless. I saw something similar in London. Maybe its a thing and I'm just too old to understand.

A bit windy

The next day I went and made my way to Arthur's seat. I didn't go alone though. Two other guys that I had just met from the hostel came along too. One fine man went by the name of Gil, but, honestly, I can't remember the name of the other one. Both were friendly though, making the trip far more enjoyable for me.

Arthur's seat is the name of the top of one of the hills on the outskirts of Edinburgh. It's a pretty popular place to hike. When I checked outside, it was cold but not really windy, so I thought it would be good to hike to the top. Remember, it was late November, so good weather is anything that doesn't kill you when you go outside.

I headed down with the guys, following the Royal Mile to the base of the mountain. It still looked OK, though it was cloudy now and didn't look like the sun would shine through any time soon. We started to hike our way up. About halfway up, I realised that I had made a mistake.

At ground level, it was not windy. Where I was currently standing, it was icy and very windy. Still, I was stubborn and decided it would be stupid to turn back. I was almost at the top. When I actually got to the top, the wind was so intense, I could barely stand straight. I tried to look around, but it was insane. My jacket was attacking me, with the hood slapping my face relentlessly. I managed to get a few photos and take in the view from the top through my screwed up eyes. What I could see was beautiful. I would love to be up there on a nice sunny day.

As I turned to see where my comrades had gone, my beanie flew right off my head. By luck, as it flew, it got caught on my very advanced iPhone 3GS which I was using to video the intensity of the weather up there. I packed my hat away for the rest of my time up there. I put on my hoodie, but even that didn't work in the end. It just blew off and then continued to slap my face about fifty times. I promised my jacket that I would leave it in a very dirty place if it did not start to behave. My jacket didn't listen. It was not the most pleasant feeling.

I made my way back down. It was slow progress, as the ice and wind kept putting us off balance. I was a lot lighter, being two months into the trip. My spending money for food had slowly dwindled. So, more than once, I thought I was just going to be blown the whole way back down to the base of the cliff. My jacket kept billowing out like a poor man's parachute as the wind hit us from behind. It felt like we had to make a forty-five-degree lean backwards in order to counteract the effect. I was so glad to get out of that wind when we reached the base.

Looking back at the top, it appeared to be totally calm up there. Almost innocent looking. I knew what was up there and watched as more people came to hike the mountain. If only they knew what fun lay ahead of them.

So....romantic?

As is the case with many cities, there tends to be one place that you keep visiting, at least in passing. For Edinburgh, that was the castle. It was right near my hostel and when I didn't want to go far, but I did want to be around some cool stuff, that is where I would go. Also, it's a big castle, so it's kind of hard to miss. So, after the windy adventure and a drink at the bar with my fellow travellers, I said goodbye to them and headed off, once more, to the castle.

As I made my way back up the Royal Mile, I saw an old man coming in the opposite direction. He had an awkward kink in his back, yet was still walking with determination. He had a cane, although he was not using it. His face was screwed up, he was breathing heavily, and he was building up a lot of snot. I thought he was sick. Maybe about to throw up even. Finally, he seemed to have enough phlegm for his liking and spat it out. He seemed relieved to have gotten the gunk out of his system.

As I passed the location, I noticed that he had spit right in the middle of a heart-shaped installation built into the road. I was confused, but a minute later, a second person spat into the heart. Curious, I decided to stay around and see what the deal was. Over the course of an hour, roughly ten people spat

The Other Side Of Travelling

on that spot as they passed. It seemed like a weird tradition, so I had to do some research. I asked the lady at the check-in desk at the hostel, and the story they gave me was amazing.

They explained that the heart marked the location of an old tolbooth where executions took place and debtors were held. That is the correct spelling for this particular building, in case you people that just bought the book to check for spelling mistakes were interested. It seems that the people of Edinburgh spit on it out of a hatred for the old building. It is also said to bring good luck to those who spit on it. Its official name is the Heart of Midlothian. Still, the best part of the story is that not everyone knows about the spitting.

Supposedly, a man (likely a tourist) took his partner to the heart and thought it would be a romantic gesture to propose to her by kneeling in the heart. If the story is true, the locals all gasped, but I guess he probably thought it was due to the romantic act itself and not due to the decades of spit piled up on the heart being transferred to his designer jeans. Maybe the locals were gasping at the thought of the large dry cleaning bill that he would need to pay for in order to get his pants back to how they were before.

It was a small reminder to do your research before attempting acts such as this. Things are not always as they appear, and while your action might be remembered for a long time, it may not be in the way that you originally intended it to be. When you are in a foreign country that you are unfamiliar with, that goes double.

Is that a sword or are you just glad to see me?

So, as I was saying, I went to the Castle regularly. One day, I stopped to look at a guy in a William Wallace outfit that was standing out the front of a tourist store nearby. He was taking photos with tourists. The store itself was selling lots of tartan clothes and all sorts of scotch whisky. The place was made for tourists and was right near the entrance to the castle. Obviously this guy had a prime location and must have been making a killing.

He had some full on replica weapons there too. The guy seemed to be enjoying it. He really was getting into character. The sword he had was huge. It was taller than me (I know, not hard, but still, impressive to me). I was not sure how he didn't get in trouble with the authorities. I guess it wasn't sharp. I eventually gathered my courage and managed to get a photo with the guy. I talked to him for a while after. His name was Adam and he was doing this on the weekends. All the money from the photos taken went to a charity for Leukaemia. He believes he has donated tens of thousands of pounds. He was a friendly guy and it was a good way to mix a love of history with helping the community.

I would actually see an article online about him a couple of years later. It seems he was popular with the ladies and they kept checking under his kilt to make sure he was a "real man". Rightly so, he was not happy about this. I hope it hasn't scared him off from his job.

After all the excitement of Edinburgh, I took a train back to Glasgow. The next step was a day tour up to the Highlands. It was great. Driving through the famous location, I saw many picturesque views. I took a boat on Loch Ness. They had the radar on just in case. Sadly, they didn't find Nessie that day.

The rest of my time in Glasgow, was much more pleasant. When I returned to the hostel, I met a great old dude with dreadlocks, named Ricky. He was courteous and we spent a lot of time at the bar, hanging out, talking music and swapping tales. He really turned my bad experience of that place into something much more awesome.

Every day, I walked around to music stores checking out the cool CDs while I waited for the day to come to fly down to England. I bought quite a lot of new CDs over those last days. All the music had to go somewhere and I couldn't carry it in my backpack, so I went to a post office to send it home to Australia.

The Other Side Of Travelling

I asked where I could get a box. The staff pointed and then off I went. I packed everything. Went to the counter and asked to pay. The fee was eighty pounds. That was way too much. I found out that the box given me was only meant for two kilo or under. It was too late to change, even if it was the staff's fault. I was travelling for another four months after I sent the package. It didn't arrive until two months after I got back. While I was glad to see the package finally arrived, I would recommend checking the weight limits before sending packages home in the future. For eighty pounds, it should have arrived the day before I sent it.

I left Glasgow the next day. Ricky was cool and walked me to the bus station. It was a really nice gesture and it made my day. I met many arseholes on my trip, but, kind people like Ricky keep my hopes up for humanity.

Daniel Greenwood

(View from Arthur's Seat)

(The "Love Heart", Royal Mile, Edinburgh)

The Other Side Of Travelling

(The Elephant House café, Edinburgh)

(View from hostel in Glasgow)

Daniel Greenwood

(Lock Lomond Highlands Trip)

(Entrance to the Highlands)

ENGLAND

Any more questions?

I spent a total of eighteen days in England on my big trip around the world. If I am to be perfectly honest with you, it was not my original intention. I wanted to get straight into mainland Europe and hit the ancient sites riddled throughout there. However, the visa requirements had me stuck and London was where I was to leave from via the Chunnel to Paris. So, there I was.

Yet, just because I wasn't originally planning to stay there, didn't mean that I was going to waste the time that I had. I went to all the typical places first on a free walking tour. I visited the Queen, went for a walk, went to Trafalgar Square. After my orientation, the real stuff begun.

First up on my list of things was the Winston Churchill War Rooms. Most of the artefacts in the museum were left in the bunker under some buildings near Parliament after the war. A few smart people decided they could make money by letting tourists check it out. I was one of the happy people willing to pay cash to see where history happened.

Whether you like the guy or not, at the end of the day, Churchill made some decisions that impacted a lot of how things are run today. To be at ground zero where those decisions were made was a thought-provoking experience. I have visited a lot of battle sites and in many cases, they are so old that it is guess work as to whether I have even found the right place.

However, there was no guess work here. I was walking in

the same footsteps that many of the leading men of England must have walked during one of the most crazy times in World History. I think the most interesting thing that I saw was a direct phone line to the American President. Being an important ally, they had to have a secure line for quick communication. However, I continue to wonder if Roosevelt was aware of Churchill sitting in a small cupboard that was converted to the purpose. The conversations that took place in that cupboard, well, must have been interesting.

After this, I visited the world famous British Museum. In hindsight, I should have planned my trip differently. I would have visited every other place in the world and then come to this Museum as the last stop. Instead, I did it the other way around. It is not that this museum is bad or anything, it is just that almost everything from everywhere was stolen (or permanently "borrowed" as it is often put) and placed in this museum. Stacks of Egyptian mummies, the Rosetta Stone, whole walls from Nineva, the Roof of the Parthenon. These things are no minor details to history. The British Museum displays all its imperialism and keeps it under the guise of preservation. As a history man however, I'll take what I can get, so I visited that and attempted to shove as much of the knowledge into my head as possible. It was too much though.

Every time I go back to London, I try to see more and more and I am yet to go there without finding something new. It is a great problem to have and keeps it from getting boring there.

I also visited the Imperial War Museum. As previously stated, I am not a man for war. Peace, Harmony and Love are where I am at. But, as war did change the course of many a history, in order for me to gather the full picture of humanity, it would be remiss of me to exclude such an important influence on the tracking of society.

Upon arrival, I checked out what was there. To be honest, there was not much around. It was being renovated and was due to close in two days for a very long time while they totally revamped the museum. I saw what I could, walking around

The Other Side Of Travelling

the exhibitions that were still open for inspection and was about to leave when I saw an elderly man standing by a table.

He had high widow peaks and short, very curly grey hair that was almost approaching a small afro. Everyone ignored him. My curiosity led me to make a beeline for the man and I soon saw that he was a volunteer for the museum. I stretched and limbered up. I closed my eyes and took a deep breath. I was ready for the marathon. My opponent did not know what he had got himself into. He smiled at me and said, "Would you like to check out some of the things I've brought with me? Perhaps, hear a few stories from the war?" I smiled and nodded. First hand sources are rare to find and always worth listening to.

He started by saying, "I was a very young man when the war began. I was far too young at the time to participate, but I do remember the bombings and going into the shelter during air raids." He also recalled the chocolate rations. He actually spent a bit of time talking about that chocolate ration. He seemed to think it was important to discuss just how little chocolate there was. What they had for a week, I, a confessed chocolate addict, often eat in an hour. Man, do I have life easy. He continued to tell all the normal things that most people want answered. He smiled at me and asked, "Any questions?"

I started to shake with excitement. This man was used to talking people to sleep. He had met his match. I started with my questions. At first, he was surprised. Then pleased. After thirty minutes, he looked desperate. I think he found the definition of too much of a good thing.

As long as he had been at the museum, I am sure he was wishing people were more interested in what he had to say. Now, he was regretting that wish. I was ready with more and more, hungry for knowledge, excited at the rare access to a first hand source, when he finally gave up. It was fair enough. I can be difficult to be around at the best of times.

I thanked him for his time and I walked away, questions still spinning, but reasonably happy. I hope that he gets more people that are excited to hear his stories. I hope I didn't scare him off from the job.

I will magically transform your wallet to empty

The next big thing I had planned to see was to check out the Harry Potter studios. The tickets were very expensive, but having grown up on the series, I thought it was worth visiting to see what was there. I took a train out of London, got off a short time later and took a giant purple bus that was waiting for us at the station to the studio.

When I arrived, I immediately began to see things from the movies. Right out the front were some chess pieces from the first movie. I was in fan boy heaven. I was one of the few adults alone on the tour. Most people there were with their kids. Travelling with a family there must have been so expensive. One ticket, at the time of me writing, cost roughly forty pounds sterling. Counting one family, they had four kids plus the two parents. All I can say, is that Warner Bros is definitely making money off of this cash cow.

The site was really well organised, as you would expect for the ticket price. You could see props and taste butter beer and all sorts of other wonderful experiences. However, it was at the exit that you saw what the monsters in the finance department of W.B. had been planning all along. It was a magical trap. The children were all excited, high off fairy dust or whatever they had been given. They had entered a world of real magic. To exit this world you had to pass through the magical gift shop.

One plastic wand, costs thirty pound. A fucking chocolate frog costs eight pound. Think about it, the kids come through, see the souvenirs. It is all so awesome and then mum and dad have to say they can't afford it. The kids start screaming and making a scene. They are not going anywhere 'til they get their Bertie Bott's Every Flavour Beans. Finally, exhausted, as the child has a tantrum on the floor next to the Hedwig soft toys, embarrassment kicks in. They want the kids to shut up. They don't care about "Potterdore" or "Sirius Snape". They just want to go home. So, they buy the stuff. The wallet groans. You can hear them on the phone to their bank as they do it. They may need to put another mortgage on their house, but that's how it goes.

I love the books, I love the movies, yet, something is not right about the whole deal. I wonder if JK Rowling knows or even cares. You would think she would intervene. She has enough money.

The Druids are back

As I spent more and more time and money in London, the ominous 21st of December 2012 approached. For those of you born in a time after this fateful day, a quick explanation is required. It was said that the particular date was predicted by the Mayans as the destruction of the Earth. I had a few doubts about the legitimacy of such a claim. What if the Mayans made a new one and we didn't find it? We buy our calendars yearly. What if they sold their calendar once every three thousand years (not the actual length of the Mayan calendar) and just never got around to buying the next one. Regardless, the hype of the day meant we had to do something cool. A few fellow travellers and I decided that if the world was going to end, the best place to be when it happened would be at Stonehenge.

So we bought the train tickets, got on and made it just in time, about an hour before closing. All the normal modes of transport were closed for the day, so the only option was a taxi ride out there. After the expensive train, the extra cost of a taxi hurt my wallet a bit. Luckily, sharing the cost with the other two travellers helped ease the burden.

We got to the entrance, paid for our ticket and got an audio guide. I never had the patience to listen to them before and I didn't do any better this time. It took me all of ten seconds to tune out and start just looking around. The rocks themselves were a let down. This is almost a guarantee when you consider the fact that they are so hyped up, that by the time you get there, there ain't that much more to see than what the pictures show you. They also seem a lot smaller in real life. All those epic photos seem to mess a little with the perspective. The science behind it is interesting though and the astrological alignment and such was impressive. The thing itself was just not as cool as I thought it would be.

However, from an archaeological point they are very curious and the debate over how the rock came to be and how it was moved from its original location is one to follow. I tell you though, I think any other day of the year would not have been as awesome as the day that we arrived.

The 21st of December was the Winter Solstice. This is big news in the Druid calendar. So when we arrived, it was not just boring tourists. There were druids everywhere. I didn't know that was even still a thing. However, it was and the druids were partying like it was 1099.

The druids that we saw were dancing, singing and had extremely interesting fashion choices. They had this one dance which they were doing with some sort of clapping sticks and twirls and all that. They seemed to look at Stonehenge with reverence. It was great. The intensity on the face of the dancers was amazing. They also had quite the crowd. There were more people looking at them than at the actual site they came to see.

The taxi was waiting for us outside, when we were done with all the rocks and such. The driver asked us how it was. We all kind of shrugged. The taxi driver said something to the effect of, "I hear that quite a lot actually." Which is quite crazy. If I was him, I would be hyping up the sight as much as possible. He made forty pounds to drive five minutes, sit still for an hour and drive five minutes back. If you were smart, you could study for a degree while doing that. We thanked the taxi guy (for that price, I think he should have thanked us), and took the train back to London.

As you all worked out, 21st of December came and went. We finished the night out on London Bridge, waiting for twelve o'clock to strike and the "danger" to be over. We are still here. The bridge is still there. So we didn't die and the world didn't end, but what a lucky chance to go and see actual druids. You're jealous. Admit it.

I thought it felt a bit drafty

Often there are particular types of stories that fall through the gaps in works like these. There are a number of things in my life that I would rather forget. When you come back from a big trip, you generally want to tell the exciting stories. The ones that make you look like Indiana Jones. It is not always the way that it turns out though. It is also important to be able to laugh at yourself. So I present to you, one of my more embarrassing moments on a trip.

I had only ten kilo in by backpack for my whole trip. I washed my clothes every five days at the hostel. I refused to be one of those travellers that you smell before you even see them. However, I was still short on supplies. Desperately short. I had one pair of jeans for the whole trip. They survived three months of intense work out. However, finally, on the 26th of December 2012, they died. Let us all take a moment to remember the fallen jeans. Done? Need more time? I know you can't rush the grieving process. OK, moving on.

More specifically, as I had bent down to pick up some washing to put into the drier, they had received a giant rip going from the top of my butt crack, all the way down to my balls. Now, certain holes are easy to hide. Others less so. This one was impossible to hide. There was nothing for it, I needed new pants. I would also have to wear the carcass that was my old jeans on the way to get some. I had known that the jeans were on their last legs for a while but had been putting off the inevitable. I was in the denial stage. After the unfortunate accident, they needed to be replaced. I'm not proud of it, but with the budget I had, the only place that was available to me was Primark.

 I managed to do OK for the first half of the journey. I sat down on the train, so no one would see the missing part of my pants. However, when I got to Oxford street, it was full of people. I realised I was going to have a problem. The day of sales was on. People who got presents they didn't like, were taking them back to stores, hoping the person that bought it for them was not around to see them do it. As I walked, every step took about five seconds. There were just so many people that there were bottlenecks everywhere, slowing down the pace. I briefly looked behind me. The people behind me had nothing to look at aside from my butt. It was cold and I had red underwear (my last clean pair) shining gloriously through the hole in the jeans. I must have looked like a baboon. It was an experience. For everyone that day. Some of them may never forget it either.

 Eventually, I arrived at Primark. I rushed to the jeans section, grabbed two pairs and did the "neck test" to see if they would fit. I had lost weight on my trip so far and was no longer sure of my size. The "neck test" worked. I got my pants, changed into them in the change room, ripped off the tag and took it to the counter. I gave them the bar code and lifted up my right leg for them to take the security tag off. They were confused. I explained that I was buying the pants I wore. They asked why. They seemed to be very suspicious, as if I was trying a kind of scam.

 So, in the middle of boxing day shopping, with a line as long as the Wall of China, I had to explain that my jeans had a huge hole, my butt was frozen solid from said hole and that I needed new pants that were significantly less holey.

 I was finally allowed to purchase my jeans and they took the tag off. With me being not so flexible, this actually took a while as I lifted my leg up onto the counter. I left and, free to look around at items, because I no longer had to hold my hands over my butt, managed to pick up a camera somewhere as my old one had broken a few days before.

What do you mean it's closed?

With not many days left in London, I took a day trip out to two towns called Battle and Hastings. The weather was not good. Late in December has its downsides when travelling in the UK. However, I wanted to see the supposed original battle site for the 1066 Battle of Hastings. I learned all about it in high school. It is slightly confusing. They think the Battle of Hastings happened in the town Battle and not in the town Hastings. Battle wasn't a town at the time of the Battle of Hastings. Battle became a town after the Battle of Hastings was won, partly to commemorate the Battle of Hastings. I wish they had picked a different name for it.

Either way, the important point is that it happened on a hill, with Harold on top and William the Conqueror at the bottom (should I have said spoiler alert before I wrote that?). Harold eventually gets an arrow in the eye, which ends the stalemate and William takes over. I mention a bit more from this battle in my visit to France. You should look up the full detail of the Norman invasion. It even involves Vikings. King Harold was the right King at the very wrong time.

Anyway, I took the train out of London and arrived at Battle. However, when I got there, I found out quickly that the site was closed. The big "closed" sign gave it away. I had come a relatively long way and decided that I would not be so easily defeated. I walked around the complex and found that, while the walls were very high at the entrance, at the back there was nothing more than a small fence. So, with no one around, I "accidentally tripped over the fence" and begun walking around the field. They had signs to explain what they thought happened where and I was brave enough to go up to the top of the hill to get a perspective from Harold's station. I also saw the ruins of a church that was supposedly built on the spot where Harold eventually died. I was not brave enough to go further afield in case there were cameras around. It was a tense moment, but, for me it was enough. I had seen the location and had my moment of history.

That was until I went back to the information station to find out that they are not even sure which hill it was. Many believe that it was the one I had just visited, with others claiming it was another hill nearby. So I visited that one too. I must admit, once I visited the second one, the trip did not feel quite as successful. I knew that I had likely visited the site. However, I was not sure which hill it was, so I left more confused than when I started. Who knows, maybe next year they think it was another hill entirely. It is all a bit unclear.

I hopped back on the train and went on to Hastings. I grabbed a quick bite to eat and then went to see another ruined castle near the beach. It was closed too, but with a small hill near the entrance, I was able to climb up and at least have a good look inside. It was supposed to be the first castle built after the victory by William, but there isn't much left. The Romans seemed to be better builders. I guess it was probably impressive at the time and the location was smart, as one could observe the happenings both at sea and on the land surrounding it comfortably. It was probably cold though and, to para-quote Blinkin, "I guess the castle must have been drafty."

I have nothing to do with this.

Not long after that, it was New Years Eve. I was originally planning to go by myself. However, just before I was going to leave, I was invited to see the fireworks from Hyde Park with some people from the hostel. One of them was a big, tall, lanky guy with gelled black hair from New Zealand. He was trying to grab the attention of a few girls. Just before we left, he drunk most of a bottle of Vodka. Maybe he thought it would reduce his nerves. It was not a good idea.

Over the course of the next half hour, his behaviour became more and more unpredictable. His ability to walk

The Other Side Of Travelling

straight also dropped substantially as we continued to move further away from the hostel. So, far as I could see, the girls didn't seem too impressed. We got to the location and the effects of the Vodka were working pretty strongly. He couldn't stand anymore. I barely knew the guy and he was too big to lift, so we lay him down and went back to looking at the fireworks. We tried to stand around him so that no one would step on him as the crowd flowed past us.

Two girls came up, both around twenty five and started having a heated discussion with us. They thought it disgraceful that we had left this guy on the ground. "What kind of friends are you?" they asked. I didn't want to lie, so I said, "Not very good ones." While it is true, I was not good friends with the guy, the girls didn't seem to think that was a great answer. As they tried to get him up and be his saviour, he freaked out.

I don't think he did it on purpose. He was so drunk I am not sure he could do anything on purpose, but when he lifted his arms in a drunken stupor, he punched both of them in the face. Hard. Right on their noses. I pictured a "boom" or a "crash" appearing, like in the comic books. There was a moment of silence as we all took stock of the situation.

Drunk man passed back out, we all tried not to laugh and the girls looked around in shock. Then, they got a second wind. The girls, were now berating us and him at the same time. It was impressive. Their skills of multitasking were exemplary. They brought police over. We managed to talk down the situation. Worst of all for me, at this point his actual friends decided to leave me and another girl with him. Not the most romantic setting. The fireworks, a cute girl, a bright-eyed Australian and a drunken, drooling New Zealand caveman. Probably the worst New Years Eve I have ever had. Though, from what I hear, this is generally how New Years Eve parties go when you try to walk in with high expectations.

A few days later, I took the Chunnel to Paris. On the train, I saw a magical sight. On every flight or long distance travel, there is always a drinker. However, here, I watched four men each put down eighty pounds for a few shots of whisky. They went back twice and did the same thing. The train left St Pancras station at 6 am in the morning. You know the saying, go hard or go home. They were going hard, but I don't think they were going home. If they kept that up, I don't know if they would remember how to get home or have the money for a ticket, even if they could. They might even have slept through their stop. I hope they ended up somewhere nice at least.

Before we move on to France, I have one more England based story. We will pick up the narrative right after this. It's my book, I do what I want.

Did someone fart?

Anyway, surely, by now you have gathered that I like history. So, it shouldn't surprise you that in October of 2015 I took a trip to the UK to see Hadrian's wall. The final frontier of the Roman Empire. Epic. You're jealous, aren't you?

I flew into Edinburgh and walked around town for an hour or two. I visited a number of my old favourite sites and also checked out some new ones. I tried to find that Wallace impersonator. I was out of luck this time and he seemed to be taking a day off. At the end of the day, I took the train down to Newcastle Upon Tyne. I stayed the night there and in the morning, took the first train out to Bardon Mill. It was here that my first real mistake occurred.

I had my full pack with me, full of supplies for the length of my trip and a fair amount of food in case I found it difficult to meet my dietary requirements. I arrived at the station. However, there was no taxi rank. There was no bus service. I was travelling outside of the standard tourist season. I would have to walk up to the wall.

It was a long journey and killed way too much time. Eventually, I got there. The fort that I visited was pretty cool. I took a taxi and visited a second fort. I walked along the wall for a while. It is a lot smaller than I imagined it. I had been told

The Other Side Of Travelling

that not much was left, but when I got there, I saw just how little remained. Even still, I could stand there and picture it in its full grandeur. Sometimes, you have to use your imagination to fill the gaps.

After I had ticked everything off from my Hadrian Wall experience, I managed to get a taxi to take me to Haltwhistle, where I stayed the night using an Airbnb, before moving on. I headed off to Carlisle and then made my way down with the train where I spent the night at Manchester. I managed to pick up some good music there from a few good second hand stores. The next day, I headed off to Bath, where I wanted to see the old Roman Baths.

Before I did that, as the baths were not open, I first took a look at the Cathedral and took a tour to the top. It gave a clear glimpse of an old town. At the roof, I got my first glimpse of the Roman Baths. I was so excited. As soon as I finished the tour, I ran down and I got my ticket, entered and made my way through the museum. There was lots of little artefacts and useful bits of information to keep me going for hours.

Eventually, the big moment arrived and I prepared to enter the bath area. To be honest, before I saw anything, I smelled it. The smell was unique. It was being heated from volcanic vents and the place was full of steam. When I finally came around the corner and saw the bath itself, the green colour of it was beautiful. Yet, not necessarily inviting for a swim. There were a few tourists and a couple of people dressed up as Romans. I figured they were employees and I approached one to ask a few questions about the bath. This was going to be my first experience with cos-players. I can't say I walked away enjoying it.

"Hello, I was wondering if you could ans..." That was all I managed to get out before the employee exclaimed "Ave fellow traveller! Have you come here for the healing waters of the Roman Bath?" I tried to play along, figuring that it would get on his good side, so said "Yes! By Jupiter, how did you get here?" He and his partner took turns explaining how they

141

made it to "Britannia". "I arrived after my import business fell through and so I made my way to Britannia to see if I could make a new life." His partner came next with his story, "I was a Roman Soldier, honourably discharged after serving on the front under one of the illustrious generals."

Hoping I had boosted their ego with this little display, I began to get down to the real questions. "When was this built?" I thought that I would start with something simple. Their response didn't give me much confidence. "We are not sure exactly. We have just arrived after a twenty day journey. The word is that it was built around ten years ago. During the rein of Emperor Claudius."

Realising that I would have to do some conversational jujitsu in order to get any information, I tried to continue. "So, how were the baths used? Was it for cleaning or social purposes?" They both looked each other with incredulity and then at me like I was an alien.

"Where *have* you been? You never been to the baths before? What kind of Roman citizen are you? Perhaps, with that beard of yours you are a barbarian. Yes, that would make more sense. They are used for both cleaning and social interactions." The second one added, in a hushed tone, "as well as business." They shook their heads at each other as if they were talking to someone beyond all hope. It was at that point I gave up and went back to reading the signs. When I turned back, they had enthusiastically trapped an elderly couple who looked thoroughly bewildered. They were showing a wax tablet and were writing Latin on it hastily to show how it could be wiped clean for reuse. I wanted to show them my smart phone, but I was afraid they might throw it in the water as a "cursed object".

The rest of the museum was well done and gave a good picture of the every day life of the people living in those times. You always read about the emperors, but a bath was something that most Roman citizens had access to, regardless of status. Which gives you a closer picture of how it really was like.

At the exit, you can try the famous water after it has been sanitised. You can't drink the liquid inside the baths, it is filled with microbes. One girl ended up dying from a microorganism infection after swimming in a pool with water from the spring. However, there are filtered and sanitised versions that you can try for yourself. It tasted horrible. No wonder people thought it must contain healing properties. It must have been useless for anything else. I flew back home the next day. It was a good trip.

Now we return to our original story, after my early morning train ride to Paris.

Daniel Greenwood

(Winston Churchill War Rooms)

(Stonehenge, 21st December, 2012)

The Other Side Of Travelling

(Section from Hadrian's Wall)

(Roman Bath, Bath)

(British Museum)

(Harry Potter Studios chess pieces from first film)

The Other Side Of Travelling

(Harry Potter Studios)

(Abbey on Senlac Hill, supposed Battle of Hastings location)

FRANCE

The Locked Away Painting

    I first arrived in Paris two days after that disastrous New Year's Eve in London (2nd of January 2013). I was lucky that a French dude I had met in Australia, called Mathias, was willing to let me sleep on the couch, otherwise there would have been no way I could have afforded to stay as long as I did. Mathias had a cool, almost afro thing going on when I met him and some neat glasses. I owe that guy big time. Mathias and another guy named Nathan took me around and showed me a few cool locations to help me get my bearings in the crazy city. Nathan had close cut brown air, was average height and had a really calm attitude to everything. Nathan even took me up to meet his parents, where we had a view of the Eiffel tower from the apartment window. I really recommend getting to know locals. It was so awesome.

    But anyway, when I first arrived at the main train station of Paris, I got off the train and was immediately bombarded by scammers. A nice, middle age French lady basically told them to fuck off and helped me through the pack. I appreciated it. I always feel super vulnerable when I have my full pack with me. It always feels like a huge flag that says, "Please steal from me." I ditch it in the hostel or locker as soon as possible and find that almost immediately, the heat dies down.

    So, after leaving the station, I started with the stereotypical things. First was the Eiffel Tower. When you arrive, you have two choices. The elevator or the stairs. I had elected to take the stairs rather than the elevator for two reasons. Reason

The Other Side Of Travelling

one: I could get a series of vantage points without the pressure and rush of tourists. Reason two: the ticket was cheaper if you took the stairs and I was poor. I like to think I was more motivated by the first reason than the second, but you never know.

Once I reached the top, I quickly discovered that, the Eiffel Tower is one of those things that is better to look at from below than to be at the top and look down. At the top, in the twilight, it was beautiful. However, the view was missing the iconic symbol of Paris (because I was standing on it). So, after climbing all that way up, doing a good once over around the top, I went straight back down, and waited for the hour to come when the tower started to light up like a psychotic, seizure inducing Christmas tree. Supposedly, it does that every hour, on the hour after dark. Ticking one of the important boxes for Paris off of my bucket-list, I made my way back to Mathias' apartment and found that my friend had made me crepes and bought me some cidre. Have I told you all yet that this guy was a legend?

The next day, I took one of the walking tours. I try to do these in every town. They are a quick way to get a good orientation of the city and see what you actually want to see. In two short hours, you can cut a lot of the crap out that would otherwise take forever to sort out, as you compare maps and plan it into your timetable, only to be disappointed upon arrival. We saw lots of cool things and I felt like I had a good understanding of the layout of the city.

On my way back, I decided to pop into one of the many churches to check it out. There was no particular reason why I picked this one over any others, only that it was there when I had decided I should look at something. It was pretty empty and when I entered I asked if I could take photos.

The priest didn't understand English. I didn't understand French. I still didn't want to get into trouble. So I pulled my camera out and pointed to it and then to the walls. I was hoping that my terrible miming skills (in a city where miming is famous) would allow us to communicate. He nodded and beckoned for me to follow him.

I didn't know where he was taking me, but I was sure that my message was totally lost in translation. However, without any common language, I didn't even know how to say stop. He pulled out a big set of keys and unlocked a door. He ushered me into this special room. I was very confused. Did I have to sign a license to take photos or something? This felt all too secretive. Then he pointed to a painting on the wall. It was beautiful.

He had interpreted my request to use a camera as a question about paintings. I don't know how he twisted my actions into paintings, but he had provided. He just seemed to be excited to be able to show someone. The painting was the 'Last Supper' by Tintoretto. I am aware that there is another version in Venice, taking on a different look and feel. However, this one is pretty good too. I'm not sure if it was a reproduction or original. I did find an article about it in the NY times, which may or may not lend credibility to its authenticity. Either way, it felt like I was in one of those Dan Brown books. I was waiting for the guy to show me that the Illuminati painted it or something. In the end, it was just the awesome painting. I left soon after, thanking the priest for taking the time to show it. I hope he understood some of it.

You never know what will happen, but giving things a go as well as interacting and being polite with the people around you can often lead to new and exciting adventures. After all this, I was exhausted and headed back for a good night rest.

It looks better on the screen

The next day, I had booked my ticket to enter the Louvre. I am not a massive art fan, but I would have been stupid not to check out the museum. It was under renovations. This is a constant struggle you must be prepared to face when travelling in the off season. However, the most famous things were still accessible.

I entered through the famous glass pyramid and moved

straight to the Mona Lisa. I figured that by a certain hour the painting would be swamped. I hoped that, by arriving at opening time and by getting there first, I may be able to actually see the painting. I was short and would not do well if there was a crowd. Europeans are tall. I ran around the corner and entered the room to find it full already. I guess everyone else had the same idea as me. We are often not as smart as we like to think.

My first impressions of the painting were that it was, well, uhhh, small. Underwhelming. Not that great. Maybe it is just my lack of understanding in art or an unfamiliarity with the style, but I really felt a bit cheated and that it was majorly over-hyped. Especially, when I turned my back and saw the beautiful paintings in the same room as its famous cousin. Compared to those around it, this was a bland, boring painting of a weird looking lady. I should have known that already. Yet, there was a bonus.

While the painting sucked, the people didn't. They were going insane over it. The best tourists had these giant iPads which they held over their face in order to get the best picture of the tiny, passive aggressive lady painting. In many cases, they couldn't see it because of the crowd and raised their iPads to get the important Instagram shot. They travelled from all around the world to see this painting. Some managed to get two metres away and not be able to see it. So, in the end they paid all that money to see a photo of a painting they could have downloaded online. You would be surprised how often that is the case.

After I was done trying to understand the Mona Lisa, I left the room and began to wander around the other galleries. The rest of the museum was cool, but as I said, not being able to tell you a thing about art, I will not write much more here. There were paintings and stuff. They were well done and often probably took a long time to do. They were also probably each worth more than I will make in my life time. Interesting visit. After the Louvre, I made my way to the Arc de Triomphe.

It's opposite day

Here was another amazing site, which was overshadowed by the surroundings. The Arc de Triomphe sits in the middle of a roundabout. The arc itself was well put together and tourists were taking happy snaps. A worthy thing to stop and take a look at, in my humble opinion. But, as I said, it was overshadowed by its surroundings.

It was the most insane thing I have ever seen on a road. I am not sure exactly what the rules are, but it seems to be that, the person entering the roundabout at the Arc de Triomphe has right of way. This goes against the convention of every other roundabout I have seen in the world. The result was chaos incarnate. There was no traffic flow. Cars stopped and started everywhere. The point of the lines separating lanes seemed to be guidelines at best, to be ignored as required. I was surprised that there wasn't a fatal auto inferno every time someone merged into the roundabout. Horns were blazing all the time. If you don't believe me, just look up footage online. Absolute craziness. I can only imagine having heart-attacks every time I would drive through it. This is definitely one to watch from the sidelines.

After the intensity of all that, the next few days were spent wandering throughout the city and purely enjoying the surroundings.

Love Unending

One thing I saw all throughout my travels were locks on bridges. You may have seen them too. They normally have the initials of the two love birds written on with a love heart. They use either white out or a permanent marker to leave their mark on the lock. The idea is that you are so committed to one another that you want to represent your relationship like a lock. When you think of the psychological meaning behind it all, it's a little disturbing. I suppose everyone has their

The Other Side Of Travelling

own brand.

I hadn't thought much about these locks as I went through the world seeing more interesting aspects. Yet, at one of these bridges, I learned to appreciate the little actions of humanity. It was a lesson that I continue to hold with me until this very day.

To set the scene for this life altering event: I was sitting on a park bench somewhere after a long day wandering through the city. It was cold and so I was huddled up on the bench, my cheap jacket and scarf wrapped tightly around me and not doing much in terms of actual protection from the weather or looking cool.

Off in the distance, I saw a couple. They were arm in arm, trying to keep each other warm. They headed towards the bridge and started leaning on the railing and chatting. I guess they were taking in the views. After a while, they turned to one another, smiled and took out a lock. Holding the lock and each taking a hand to lock it on the bridge, they smiled, kissed each other passionately and stared lovingly into the eyes of each other. They threw the key into the water and then went on. I saw them fading off into the distance. I had never seen the full ritual before and was in the process of analysing its finer points and metaphorical meanings. I was also thinking that they had picked a good bridge. Many of them are covered with locks. This one was relatively sparse by comparison.

It was then that I saw the life changing moment. A construction worker for the city came by. He went to the bridge too. He too leaned on the railing and looked out into the distance. He had a cigarette in his hand and was clearly in deep thought. I was guessing to myself, thinking of all the possible reasons for this visit. Had he lost a loved one and this was where they had put their lock? As if in answer, he started looking around the locks, reading this one or that. With such comparatively few locks, I was sure he would find what he was looking for. Finally, he located it. He had a huge smile on his face.

With slow, deliberate movements he took something out of his backpack. I couldn't see it at first. However, eventually, I got a clear view. He had taken out a bolt cutter, placed it on the lock of his choice and cut it off. He moved to the next one and cut it off too. The smile widened. I watched him work until I couldn't feel myself from the cold. That smile, that moment of bliss of the man, enjoying his work, was one that I will remember forever.

It makes sense though. It's about structural integrity of the bridge. That bridge must have been more than one hundred years old. There is no way that the architect sat there and thought about how their shining piece of work was one day going to have to carry an extra one thousand kilograms of steel from all the people putting their unique acts of love next to all the other unique acts of love, weighing down and ultimately destroying the bridge. I don't think they built in the strength for that kind of act. I actually read that the main bridge in Paris where people had been doing this was close to collapse and the workers had to pull whole panels of the bridge off to repair the damage done from these locks.

Put your lock somewhere actually relatively stable. Like space.

The Other Side

After all this, I gave Mathias a break from me sleeping on the couch. I managed to make my way up for a few nights in Bayeux, in Normandy. It had been high up on my list for a while and I had just decided to go for it. Trouble was, there is not much up there in the way of accommodation. Sure, if you can pay, you will find a nice quaint hotel with good food and wine. However, that was not something I was able to do. Money prevented me from the standard accommodation and I doubt I would have paid for it even if I could. I managed to find an Ibis Hotel that was supposed to be nearby the station in Bayeux. I took the train from Paris and proceeded to walk,

The Other Side Of Travelling

following the directions on my map. It was not close. It was dark before I got to the darn hotel. The bed was comfortable though.

Being a history nut, I wanted to check out the Bayeux tapestry. I have to say, for something that is almost over one thousand years old, it still looks pretty good. About seventy meters long in a dark room you follow the story of William and Harold as they battle it out for supremacy of England. **Spoiler Alert**: In case you forgot, Harold gets hit in the eye with an arrow. As far as I know, that is generally not a good sign if you want to be a winner. Sure enough, William ends up winning the battle and becomes William the Conqueror. He created the Doomsday book which is essentially a tax book. I think they should keep using this name for all taxes. I was glad I saw the tapestry, as it created the full loop between my visit to Battle and Hastings in England.

The other major reason for being up there, is Bayeux was not far from the D-Day landings in World War II. I arrived in December, so like all tourist destinations during winter, the bus to the beach was not running. I would have to use my non-existent French and pointing to find the directions to the beach. I would take my hired bike for the twenty kilometres ride.

Setting off with only a general direction as my guide, looking for sea gulls or other signs of sea life to help me, I quickly noticed a problem. Every time a car went past, I had a minor heart attack. Pedalling, peddling, ARGH! That is the precise moment I remembered Australians drive on the other side of the road. This was not going to be easy. While I continued to feel my heart muscles seize, I spotted something off in the distance that distracted me.

It was a guy on a bike. Normally, people on bikes in the country look reasonably relaxed. The nice air, open spaces lend themselves for a relaxed journey. This guy however, did not look relaxed. In fact, he looked even worse than I did (which at the time was very difficult). Every time a car passed him, he swerved so violently I thought he would launch straight into the car. He had a red North Face jacket on and blond curly hair. I had a theory that popped into my head, but I wanted to confirm it.

So, picking up the pace as fast as my untrained legs would let me, I caught up to him. On a whim, I said 'G'day mate'. He responded in kind. All fell into place. He was a fellow left hand side of the road driver. I had found in the middle of a remote part of France, the only other guy crazy enough to be riding a bike that day to see the beach. He was Australian. It seems that wherever I go there are the locals, plus an Australian and a pair of fifty year old Germans.

Luckily for me, he had GPS with him, so following him, I was able to finally get to the beach. There were lots of little signs that we were approaching the battle site, with war cemeteries popping up more and more often. About one kilometre out from the main entrance, the front tire of my companion's bike burst. Figuring that we would deal with this later, we went and checked the beach out.

It was, to sum it up in one word, surreal. A lot of the bunkers are still there and you can climb into them. I tried to get a glimpse of an idea of what the landing parties might have dealt with, by running from the shore line with my pack to the cover of the dunes. It was hard. The sand was fine and my boots immediately sank in upon impact. I knew war sucked before this moment and I sure as hell don't agree with violence. However, running along that beach, I was even more sure. I was tired before I even reached halfway. I would have been picked off within seconds.

The other interesting point to note is how the different countries dealt with their dead. The American graves were uniform and immaculate. Name, number, religion, perhaps a date of death. Row after row of white crosses, Stars of David and Crescent Moons were before my eyes. It was overwhelming. The British quarters were not so organised. Notes from parents were written on the tomb stones. I think both have their merits. It was chaotic but felt more real. The British quarter definitely made me feel the humanity of it all, while the American side gave me a glimpse of the sheer numbers involved. Either way, this type of war is something I hope never happens again. Sadly it slowly seems to be heading this way but I hope it can be resolved.

After we had seen our fill of everything, we decided to head back to Bayeux. We caught a taxi back because of the tire and split the bill. That evening I went back to Paris, to meet Mathias and Nathan. The day after that, I continued my journey through Europe.

Daniel Greenwood

(Eiffel Tower with added seizure inducing display)

The Other Side Of Travelling

(The Louvre)

(Omaha Beach, Normandy)

Daniel Greenwood

(American Grave Site, D-Day landings)

(Quai des Orfevres near the Sainte Chapelle. Bullet holes from retaking of Paris in WWII)

The Other Side Of Travelling

(Roundabout at Arch de Triomphe)

(Notre Dame in better days)

ITALY

Is the toilet leaking?

As I continue to mention, I am a bit of a history nerd. As such, for pure accessibility of artefacts, there are few better places to be, for someone like me, than in Italy. I took the overnight train from Paris to Venice. The idea was to save time by travelling while I slept, waking refreshed and getting straight into the action upon arrival at my destination. It did not all go to plan. I did not get a single wink of sleep.

An old guy, among others was sharing the cabin with me. He was rather tall, skinny but with a beer belly and with wispy white hair styled into a relatively neat hairstyle. He was sleep walking and talking. The whole. Damn. Night. If this was a dormitory, it might not be so bad. However, he was doing this in a small two by two meter cabin on a speeding train. As if the sleep muttering was not enough, he also turned the heater up to thirty degrees. Way too hot in such a small cabin with no breeze and six people sleeping. I swear I nearly died of dehydration. I was also worried I was giving a sweat shower to the person in the bed below mine. It was just that hot and stuffy in there. As horrible as that was, it was worth it in the end though. I arrived, with bloodshot eyes and dishevelled hair at Venice main station and started checking out the sites.

I started with taking a boat bus to my hostel. The hostel was near to San Marco Square which was convenient and had a little supermarket nearby for supplies. The guy that ran it wanted to be friends with everyone.

Whenever you would walk into the hostel, he would call you in from reception, ask you about your day, have a small peak of what you were cooking and then send you on your merry way. He always looked so proud of himself. The smile said, "Look, I am interacting."

A tiny bit of the experience for a tiny bit of time.

After checking in, I walked to San Marco Square and then did a loop through the major sites. It was all very beautiful and because I was there in winter, there were very few people and the water didn't stink. So I had that going for me.

One thing that everyone should do though is get a gondola ride on the canals. That is what you do in Venice, right? It's romantic and wonderful and so scenic. That will set you back up to eighty euros. Probably more in peak season. I just did not have that kind of money. Yet, I did want the experience. So I took the backup option. Near San Marco Square is a stretch of water with no bridge. Almost all other crossings between segments of Venice have a bridge nearby. However, the nearest crossing from St Mark's to the island opposite is quite a walk away. The water way is rather wide there and a bridge would be impractical to build. As a result, someone, perhaps the government, provides a service. For two euros you can sit in a boat paddled by two men from one side to the other. The ride is not long, a minute or two at the most. Though, if you are on a tight budget, it counts. It's not the length, it's how you use it, right?

I took the gondola ride and tried to enjoy it as much as I could. However, it was pretty quick and with the waves and such, well, not so smooth as you see in the movies. After all was said and done, I then walked around that segment of the city. I took the long way back to the main square and when I did, it looked entirely different. There were platforms being built everywhere. Hovering walkways filled the square and surrounding streets. They had popped up in the space of about an hour. The workers looked like they were all competing in a race against time to finish the job. As I came round the bend to arrive back at where I had left on the gondola ride, I saw why.

The tide was coming in. Fast. With it the water level was rising and engulfing the square and surrounding area. It seems that around certain particularly high tides, the square and other sections of Venice get flooded, which means that the only way for the people to still get around in their designer shoes is to use these raised pathways. An interesting solution, perhaps they can find a better one soon. I doubt it, though.

The other thing, aside from the canals, that you can do is see the glass blowers. They are famous and the glass pieces of Venice, when done well, are real masterpieces. They advertise free demonstrations of how glass-blowing works. Essentially, it is a ten minute presentation and a not so gentle nudge (it felt more like being herded) into the gift shop, where you can buy your glassware. Worth checking out, but don't expect an in-depth scientific explanation of glass blowing, the temperatures and how the colours are introduced. Expect "Look, isn't it pretty? Want to buy it?" I guess they got to make their money, right?

Also, just be aware of how much space you take up with your backpack. It would be a shame to end your trip because all your budget was blown to pay for that blown glass you broke. See what I did there? "Blown." I crack myself up. I'm sorry, I love a good pun. I'm back in control now. All I meant to say was that you would be shattered to have destroyed all the glass. OK, OK. I'm stopping now.

Venice is not a big place, and within two days I had checked out a great deal of what was to be seen on my limited budget. There were of course lots of cool things outside my budget, such as some of the more expensive museums and such. If I ever go back, I would love to check them out.

Did you check the forecast?

I had bought an unlimited rail pass before arriving in Europe, so I decided to use the opportunity in Italy to visit the three major battle sites of Hannibal of Carthage. Isn't that what you all would do? You have the whole of Italy at your feet. Bologna, Milan, these cities are nothing. You want to see ancient battle sites. That is where the really good stuff is. No, it's only me? Damn.

One site, in the surrounding hills of Lake Trasimeno was a simple train ride, remote but relatively easy to get to from Florence. The others, however, would be remote and difficult to find. I never managed to go to the site of the massive battle at Cannae. I did try to get to the location on the river Trebbia though. Through research I discovered, that the Romans had retreated from the battle to a town called Placentia (now called Piacenza), so I took the train from Venice and started there.

When I arrived, it was snowing. I was not prepared for this kind of weather. I had left sunny Venice and made the poor assumption that all in Northern Italy would be similarly pleasant. Even still, with my poor choice of clothes, I decided to stay. Thinking it would be OK and keeping a positive attitude, I started to move. Listening to the podcast story of the battle of Trebbia (by the great Dan Carlin), I was walking through the town. It was nice enough. I did not have a map and perhaps for the only time in my travels, I got hopelessly lost. That is of course not to say that I have never been lost. However, most other times, it was minor details. I was one street over from where I should be or had taken a left instead of a right and was able to easily retrace my steps.

This was different. I didn't speak Italian and the town was remote enough that English was not a major language that they were used to experiencing. I tried my broken Portuguese, hoping that the closeness of the languages might lend some understanding. That did not work either. I had not paid enough attention to where I was going and now I was in trouble.

The worst bit about it was that I should have known better. The battle itself is famous because it took place during the winter months, it was snowing and Hannibal took advantage of the weather by making the Roman soldiers go through the icy cold river before beginning. The whole point of why the site was famous is the snow and I, arriving at the town around the same time of year, was surprised to see snow. I spend a lot of time trying to make myself smart. However, moments like that show that I still have a very long way to go.

The snow was leaking into my shoes. It was soaking my pants. I was frozen solid. Defeated, I just wanted to make the two hour train ride back to Venice. But I couldn't find the station. I walked around for a long time. Finally, with the help of a local who managed to correctly interpret my very accurate "Choo Choo Train" sign language, I eventually found it. The closest I got to the battle site was the connection of the Trebbia to the Po river. Due to my poor navigation skills, I got the smallest glimpse of what that might have felt like to be out in that cold. I would not get lost like that again. I hoped.

When I got to the train station, I had a few options. Option one was to take a four hour train ride and arrive well after dark. The other was an express train. I decided that I would take the express and hoped that I wouldn't get kicked off. It was the better option, but I was concerned because my unlimited train ticket didn't cover these express trains without a charge. A charge that I couldn't afford.

I found a whole empty carriage, dimmed the lights, took my shoes and socks off and cranked the heater in an attempt to dry them and my feet a bit. Just as they went from "soaked in a pool" wet, to "just through the spin cycle" wet, the ticket inspector came. She asked for my ticket. I smiled and showed her my unlimited pass. She told me my ticket didn't cover it. I tried to look cute and say that I didn't know that and asked if

I could stay as it was so empty anyway. She said no and kicked me off the train. I should have realised that with how I looked, shoes and socks off, shaggy beard, ripped clothes and my generally dishevelled appearance, I would not be able to managed cute. I could probably have managed homeless. However, I don't think that would have helped me either.

I put my wet socks and shoes on (oh how I hate that feeling) and got off the train at the next station. I think I nearly cried. I remember being very emotionally drained. It is funny what things get to you. The next train came, and by luck would only take another hour, but I couldn't find a spot with a heater for my shoes and so sat there in my wet clothes for the rest of the journey. When I finally limped into my hostel back in Venice, the guy at the desk took one look at me, went to ask his usual questions, but hesitated and let me go. I looked defeated and spent the rest of the evening, wrapped up in the covers trying to get the feeling back in my limbs.

You don't like my chocolate.

I took one more day trip out from Venice. It was the day after Piacenza. I don't know how I managed to get out of bed. My whole body ached. Yet, this was a once in a lifetime trip and so I dragged my sorry self out, put my *almost* dry clothes on and hit the road.

This time, the destination was to a town called Verona. The city is nice and it seems to be linked to the story of Romeo and Juliet. I just can't quite follow how. The purpose of my visit was, of course, to see the Roman Amphitheatre. Better preserved than the Colosseum, and less crowded with visitors, it would be a neat introduction to Ancient Roman architecture.

I once again took the train and sat there looking out the window, taking in the various sights. I was absorbed in another one of Dan Carlin's epic podcasts. At some point, an elderly lady sat nearby. She was skinny, with sagging cheeks and her dark grey hair was pulled back into a very tight bun that stretched her forehead a bit. I smiled at her and she smiled back. I struggle to ignore people and it often gets me into weird situations. As has previously been mentioned, I didn't know any Italian.

The lady said something to me. A few of the words were reasonably recognisable. Others, I could kind of gather from my Portuguese knowledge. After a short pause to process, I worked out that she was offering me chocolate. While I was working it all out, she had pulled out a block of chocolate.

I politely declined. She insisted. I tried to explain that I was allergic to gluten and the particular chocolate she was offering me unfortunately contained that particular chemical which made my bowels explode. She looked at me confused for a while. Had my message got through? Was my use of Portuguese enough to get the explanation of my medical condition through. Finally, she looked at me and said something to the effect of "You just don't like my chocolate." She looked a combination of hurt, disappointed and annoyed. She turned away.

I felt bad and hadn't meant to upset her, but I really would have been sick. I couldn't afford any days of diarrhoea, no matter how nice the lady seemed. I smiled at her again as I left to get off in an attempt at a peace offering. She was not happy.

I actually bumped into her two more times while I was in Verona. Each time, she looked at me like I had stolen her children. I could feel her eyes burning holes in my head each time that I passed her. Never piss off an Italian Momma.

The arena was pretty cool to check out and I read somewhere that it is still used for concerts occasionally. I struggled to get the theme song from "Gladiator" out of my head. Good film, but I was trying to keep it real. Damn you pop culture and your catchiness. Well worth the visit if you can get to it.

You want your what in my what?

After my time in and around Venice, I took the train to Florence. What a place to explore. It has a cool leather market and about a million replicas of David around the city. If I go back, I want to count them and see how many I can find.

After I had taken a free walking tour to orientate myself, I visited the original David statue. It was very well done and much bigger than I pictured it. If that was how tall David was, I don't want to see Goliath. Though, his penis was really as small as everyone says. It made sense though, I could see the fear in his eyes. Introduce me to the man that doesn't have ball shrinkage when facing someone literally ten times their height and I'll be impressed. While you are at the David, make sure to check out the unfinished pieces that "guard" the David. They are so interesting to see and you can picture the figures trying to break free of the marble.

After that, I climbed up the Duomo to get a good view and checked out some of the other sites. The next day, I decided to take the train out to Pisa and Cinque Terra. The town of Pisa is reasonably famous and I don't think I need to do much explaining there about what I was going to see. Cinque Terra are five very small but beautiful villages on the coast. A must visit for good views, food and a bit of relaxation.

However, I am already getting ahead of myself. Let me tell you first about my time in Pisa. That town was not relaxing. I was hesitant to go there. Even this time of year, during winter, when tourism was low, I was sure the leaning tower would not be empty. When I arrived early in the morning, at 8 am, my theory was confirmed. It was absolutely packed. I took a few snaps before more people flooded the area and looked around.

I have to admit, I spent most of my time watching the people. The tower was OK. The people, however, were way more fascinating. A lot of them were doing "that thing". You know, where you take a photo of you pretending to hold up the tower in order to stop it from falling. Not necessarily unique, but fun. A photo you can send home to your grandma. Not everyone was doing the standard shot though. There was a group of people, off in the distance, doing quite different poses. They were using the Tower in a more creative fashion.

It started with the gentlemen. They each got down, in turn, on the ground, raised their pelvis. They made it look like the Pisa was an extension of their body. Let me put it bluntly. If their appendage was that size, it would not fit into their pants and the amount of blood that would be needed to erect that tower does not exist in any animal that is living today. However, the most graphic was yet to come.

It started with one of the females getting down on the floor on all fours. Raising her high butt into the air and lowering her head close to the ground, she started making an "O" face at the camera. From the right angle, which her photographer was expertly taking photos from, the Leaning Tower of Pisa looked as if it was entering her, very painfully, from behind where the sun doesn't shine. If that was not enough, a second girl stood behind her. By raising her hands in a particular fashion, which at first looked like some kind of waltz, she was able to make it look as if she was placing the tower into her friend. The friends that play together, stay together…right? Charming poses.

I took a gamble. I had an idea of where they might be from. But, ever the scientist, I had to test the theory. Casually, as I walked passed, I said "G'day." They responded in kind. Internally, I sighed. Australians have a reputation for being fun to be around, nice, easy going and adventurous. While that is good for the most part, it does also result in the above mentioned situation. Australia has its fair share of interesting representatives. Our understanding of public decency has got us into trouble in other countries more than once. After chatting with the group for a while, I headed back to the train station to start the next part of the journey.

Cinque Terre was beautiful, but ultimately uneventful. I

did meet a friendly couple, a gentleman named Robert and his wife, from Malta along the way and we got to hang out and swap stories. It was wonderful to hear from someone other than my headphones for a while. If you get the chance, you should go check it out though. Seriously do it. Go! You have to! I watched the sunset in one of the towns and then headed back to my hostel. After all those adventures and a few more days in Florence soaking up the atmosphere, I continued on my journey and made my way to the mighty Rome.

Art with attitude

Rome is crazy. Lots of stuff to see. If you like shopping, you will have no trouble finding something cool. If you like history, you will have a lot of trouble deciding where to go first. The biggest trouble you will have is looking at your wallet, realising you can't do everything and having to choose. Ultimately, like I assume most people do, I made a beeline to the Colosseum and Roman Forum. Unlike most people, I found a tour that takes you both under the Colosseum and up to the third floor. In fact, only one tour does this (at the time of writing). If you find a tour that does not take you to the underbelly of the Colosseum, it is not the one to take. Some of the coolest stuff is under there. Plus, it is the only tour that allows you to stand where the gladiators actually fought.

The tour ticket also gains you access to the Roman Forum. You can still supposedly see the location where Julius Caesar was cremated. Morbid I know, but, for better or worse, that guy changed the course of the western world. I read a lot of books, but it is always better to visit the actual sites, get a 3D perspective and take in the smells and other aspects that can't be obtained from reading alone.

There are lots of other things to check out. The Vatican for example. That place had so much stuff. This made me really excited and so angry at the same time. They must have millions of dollars worth of statues (priceless in fact) and they have destroyed all of them by putting little leaves on the genitals. I don't necessarily want to see a bunch of two thousand year old marble penises. Yet, it is part of the artistic style of the time and when they added those leaves, in many cases, they seem to have damaged the original.

In fact, the mark of the Church is everywhere in Rome. On Egyptian Obelisks, Roman Victory Columns, anywhere a cross could be put on, was done so. It is said that one particular Pope (I think it was Pope Sixtus V) went round and simply blessed everything so it wouldn't get destroyed. If that is the case, we have that guy to thank for a lot of what you can see in Rome today.

While I found all the ancient statues amazing, I went to the Vatican to see the Sistine Chapel. This is where I discovered, that there are a lot of rumours surrounding a number of the more famous artists and rebellion against the Popes. The chapel is no different. You are not allowed to take photos. However, if you go there, look at the most iconic painting. It is almost in the middle of the chapel roof. There is a divider in the room and if you push your way through the crowd until you are almost there, then look up, you should be close. It is tough to verify, yet, it appears that God is sitting in the silhouette of a brain. We know that Michelangelo studied anatomy and would have known what a brain looks like. So, some interpret this as him stating that God is in the mind. People got killed for saying stuff like that before, so if this is true, Michelangelo was a bad-ass.

One of the more surprisingly interesting things I saw, as I wandered through the ancient streets of the eternal city, were the fountains. Artists were commissioned to make them. There were battles and feuds and petty infighting for the honour of the top locations. To this day you can see it. One statue that was forced to be placed in a manner that it faced a statue of a rival artist looks away in disgust. They put their grudges in stone. These artistic types seem to have strong emotions.

One guy, if the rumours are true, went even further. You

never know whether this is true or not, but there is a tale that one artist got too famous for the Pope's liking. In an attempt to take him down a notch or two, the Pope forced him to make one of the smallest fountains in Rome. It lies in the corner of a square with a gigantic fountain in the middle. Most people walk past it. It is a fountain of a clam with bees flying around it (the animal of this particular pope). If you take a closer look, it is said to resemble that of a females nether regions. The tale goes that the model used for the inspiration was in fact the Pope's sister. The Pope, with his vow of celibacy, was either unable to identify or unwilling to admit that he could identify the anatomical piece. So there it stays 'til this day.

I don't know if that is true, or if it is just what the guide told the group as a way to spice up the tour. I can't find much information verifying the story itself, so I guess you should check it out and be the judge. The fountain was made by Bernini and if you want to see it, it's in a square on Via Vittorio Veneto, a relatively short distance away from the Trevi Fountain. It is also near the Capuchin Monastery, which for some of the more morbid travellers may be of interest.

Speaking of the Trevi Fountain, I threw a coin in, so I am supposed to be able to return. I did so a year later, so definitely works. I do the hard research, so you don't have to.

Sorta, Maybe, Sorta, Maybe, I Guess

While I was in Rome, I wanted to check out St Paul's Cathedral. If you are interested and decide to go there, make sure to go to the Vatican website and find the information on the tour to go underneath the Cathedral. There is a whole Roman town there. You actually have to email the Vatican for permission and state your nationality and such. I wish the Vatican was not in as much control of all this, but there are good things to see.

When I went under, I saw lots of wonderful things, even though the lighting was not great. It was a whole set of Roman buildings under there. Amazing. But, I have to admit, the lady running the tour was quite annoying after a while. It was a mix of archaeological stuff and religious. I should have been prepared, but I wasn't. While I understand, given the location of both, that there had to be an incorporation of the Christians' roles in the Roman empire, it was her hesitation to commit to her story that caused me real frustration.

The confusion built to a crescendo as we arrived at the mythical location of St Peter's bones. She used so many "maybes" and "perhaps" that I felt like she was just making it up as she went along. I would have been more understanding if she had just said "See that bone there? The small one you can see if you look through the gap in the wall? No? Too bad for you, that is St Peter. Move on heathen."

Instead, it was more, "We think, maybe, that it might just maybe be the bones of the Saint Peter. I choose to believe that it might perhaps just maybe be true and if it is maybe true then I choose to believe it. But, you maybe sort of don't believe it and that is OK too. But maybe it is true, maybe."

At the end of the day, we were where we were. I could not see this without her, so I had to endure it with her. It would have been fine to be direct. Trust that people are able to make up their own minds. Luckily, even if the guide is not sure, the location is cool enough to make up for it.

One hell of a road to travel on

The final thing in Rome that I checked out before heading to Naples was the Appian Way. This is the old highway of Rome. When they said all roads lead to Rome, this was one of the main entrances that many travellers would have come down before entering the city. They have a stretch that is still relatively well preserved that you can visit. It is about twenty kilometres long and there is no entrance fee. My two favourite things, history and cheap. It sounded like just the thing for me.

I got to the location and hired a bicycle from a shop near

the start of the ancient road. I thought it would be a nice adventure. The last time I had ridden a bike was in France to Omaha beach, and the weather was much nicer there in Italy. Unlike my overcast adventure, this time it was sunny with a blue sky shining back at me as I started. The first part of my journey was a normal asphalt road, but eventually, car traffic stopped and the real deal began.

I'm not sure what took notice of the change first, my eyes or my backbone. I should have thought ahead of time, but a two thousand year old road is not exactly well maintained. Even with modern bike suspension, it was one bumpy ride. I tried riding on the road, I tried riding on the side of the road. It didn't matter. Everywhere I was, there were bone shattering bumps to be dealt with. It was worth it though, seeing all the interesting ruins on the sides of the road, without tourists. In fact, I was the only one there that I saw on my whole bike ride. There was one small problem though. Even when I got off the bike, I felt like I was still shaking.

Some of my favourite things that I saw were a few old road side tombs and an aqueduct. The tombs were elaborate and seemed to say a lot about the mentality of many of the people living in ancient Rome. It was not just death, it was a last chance of promoting a brand. Famous people listed their deeds on the side, proclaimed their lineage and other crazy things. Some of them were very, very big or mounted on top of small hills. Others were modest. Still, big or small, you have to remember these are on the main highway of the ancient times. Thousands of people would pass these all the time. It was important to look good.

I returned the bike back at the rental place after my journey and my butt hurt for a day or two after, but that didn't stop me from packing my bag and getting ready for the next stop on my journey, Naples.

Daniel Greenwood

The best deal in the world

Before we move on to Naples, there is something I want to mention. There seems to be a sort of strange touristy stuff Mafia throughout Italy. I know for a fact, that at the Colosseum, each dressed up Gladiator has their place. If they step over the line into the territory of someone else, you might see something reminiscent of the ancient pass time. There are also groups of people that, during the day, sell slime that splats on the ground and reforms and, during the night, sells glowing helicopter like things that are shot into the air with slingshots. There is another group that sells fake Versace hand bags. They spread their wares out on a blanket. I had seen them everywhere around the place and figured it was to protect their goods from potential destructive dog poo. In fact, it was something more ingenious.

I discovered the use of the blanket while having a hot chocolate in a café near the Vatican walls. The people were all lined up with their blankets and bags. All of a sudden, there was a sound of a siren. It took no more than two seconds and about twenty people and their "shops" disappeared in the crowd. By grabbing the four corners of the blanket they had gathered their wares, slung it over their back and ran for it. They were all laughing.

Eventually, it was clear that the police were not coming this way. So, walking back to their position, laughing at the ridiculousness of the situation, the bags went down and they were back, as if nothing had happened. I wonder how many times they have to make that manoeuvre a day? They did seem to have a lot of practice.

The offer too good to be true

I took the train from Rome to Naples, which was pretty relaxed. When I arrived in Naples though, it was like I had entered an entirely other world. Rome was a little sketchy at times, but overall very touristy. Naples is rough. Graffiti is sprayed all over the trains, including the windows. Not the good kind of graffiti either. There are no Banksy works on the train. It is all a horrible mess. The streets are less clean, rougher and the people are more intense. I was nearly assaulted for money as I stepped off the train.

Now, I don't want to give the wrong picture about Naples. There are lots of cool things to do and see (we will talk about that in a moment). All I am saying is that Naples is a tough town and can be a shock to arrive to after the relatively tourist friendly Rome.

Here is a perfect example. I am walking down the street and out of nowhere, a guy on a moped comes off the street and pulls up in front of me. He is blocking me from going further. I have no clue what is going on and am getting ready for any scenario. Is he going to steal my wallet? Assault me? He looks at me and then smiles. "Want an iPhone? A hundred euros?" I had heard of the scam before. I was not expecting to walk straight into it so soon.

It works something like this. Firstly, Moped Boy, as I shall now call him, shows you a real, genuine iPhone. This is important. People like to see the product they buy. After that, price is negotiated. Moped Boy wants to make it clear that this is a serious deal. The scammer goes to the effort to make it as legitimate looking as possible. Finally, the price is agreed on. You hand the money. He goes to give you the phone, but then remembers, a phone without a charge cord is useless. He places the phone in its original box with cords and everything and gives it to you. Then he drives off. Fast.

It feels like it has an iPhone in it, however, in reality it is just rock salt. Or sand. Though you didn't notice, when he put the phone in the box, he was actually switching boxes and giving you a dud. You have been scammed. As he is on a moped, there is no possible way of catching him. Moped Boy is already gone down a million windy side streets.

At least you have something to help your dinner taste good tonight. It might get rid of the sour taste of losing all that cash. Unless you got the sand.

Surprise Finds

Another example of how rough this place is, can be gathered by simply looking at the cars on the street. I don't think I saw one car that was undamaged, the whole time I was there. There were even two hundred thousand dollar cars with both the front and rear bumpers completely ripped off. Seeing all this carnage, I started to investigate how it all happened. I watched the streets, but, could not see any major crashes. My next guess was parking. It was there that I found the evidence I required to make a fair conclusion.

Cars would "gently" nudge one another out of the way to make space for them to park their car on the road, on the sidewalk, forward, backward, sideways, anyways they could get in. Parking is limited in this old town, so people take what they can get. The streets are narrow and the road signs are rarely followed. It is chaos and I loved it. Insurance must cost a fortune in that town. It is almost a guarantee that something will get destroyed.

In terms of the most prominent site in Naples, I didn't get to climb Mt Vesuvius due to bad weather. I tried to go up three times, but they just would not let me pass. I did go to Pompeii though. There was nothing that would have stopped me visiting Pompeii. It was amazingly well preserved and a big highlight for a history buff like me.

Luckily, I didn't go there alone. I had a tall French Canadian guy that I met in the hostel, who came along with me. His name was Guillaume and he must have been around two metres tall. I could imagine how you could be intimated by the dude, but after about two seconds, you would soon realise, he is a gentle giant. More than once, I caught him somewhere in Pompeii, standing there with his eyes closed and his hand on a stone, just trying to fully experience his surroundings. He was great company and made my time in Naples a far more interesting experience.

As almost every tour to Naples will take you to Pompeii, and nothing of note happened to me, besides perhaps hyperventilating over the frescos that still maintained vivid colour, I will leave the description of these places to your imagination and enjoyment.

One thing I can highly recommend though, is an underground tour of Naples. You are looking for one that does the following. The tour starts by going down a series of steep steps. They give you a candle to help you see what is going on. The place underground was a water reserve and even an ancient cistern. At some point, it was used as protection from bombs during WWII. You have to squeeze your way through very narrow channels and the candle thing makes it all very eerie. Guillaume came along for that too. He did struggle a bit to get through some of the sections because he was so tall. However, if he managed to get through, I think anyone can. While all that is cool, it is the next part that you have to see.

After you are done going through the underground, you are taken back above ground and through some back alleys. After what seems like forever, your guide knocks on a random door. The "owner" of the house lets you in. It all looks like a normal house. The room is rather small. There were paintings and other bits and pieces that you would normally expect. But, once everyone on the tour has entered the building and you are feeling a little cramped and confused, you are led further in. There is a wooden door on the floor which the owner lifts up. You are taken into a basement. It is there that you see it.

As you climb down a number of stairs, you see an exposed wall in the basement. Instead of a modern construction, you can now see the wall of a Roman amphitheatre. How crazy. It seems that the guy was expanding his basement and found the walls. If that doesn't give credentials to the age of the city, I don't know what does.

Daniel Greenwood

I don't understand, but thank you

As I write this, I have a book sitting next to me. I was given this book by its author while staying in the hostel in Naples. Over the time I was there, when I got back to my room, she would be there, on the bed in the diagonally opposite corner of the room. Her English was OK, but not great and admittedly, most of our conversations involved pointing at things, pulling silly faces and laughing. Sounds weird at first, however, when you think about it, is it really any worse than most other conversations you have had in the past week? In fact, I might be able to argue that it was better than most of them.

Anyway, on my last day, she stopped me as I was heading out and had the book in her hand. She said that it has poems in there that she had written. She wanted to thank me for making her feel more welcome. She explained it was a welcome change to see a smiling face everyday. So she signed and gave me the book. I was shocked, but thanked her profusely. I was not expecting anything like that. It was such a kind gift. The act was so unexpected that, at first, I didn't even look at the book. I was spending most of my time looking at the big smile on her face.

After I had left and took the train back to Rome, I pulled the book out. It was then that I realised that I couldn't understand a single word. The poems were all in Italian. The cover art is so odd that I cannot even read the title. The author is Barbarah Guglielmana. I hope I can find an Italian speaking person one day to translate some of it for me. If you know her work, let me know what it is all about, I'm interested.

Overall, Italy was a great place to visit. Crazy, with old and new mixed in to every street corner. One of my favourite countries. Check it out.

The Other Side Of Travelling

(Flooding in Piazza San Marco)

(Snow in Piacenza)

(Verona Arena)

(Appian Way)

The Other Side Of Travelling

(St Peter's Basilica)

(The interesting fountain)

Daniel Greenwood

(Leaning Tower of Pisa)

(Cinque Terre)

The Other Side Of Travelling

(Pompeii and Vesuvius)

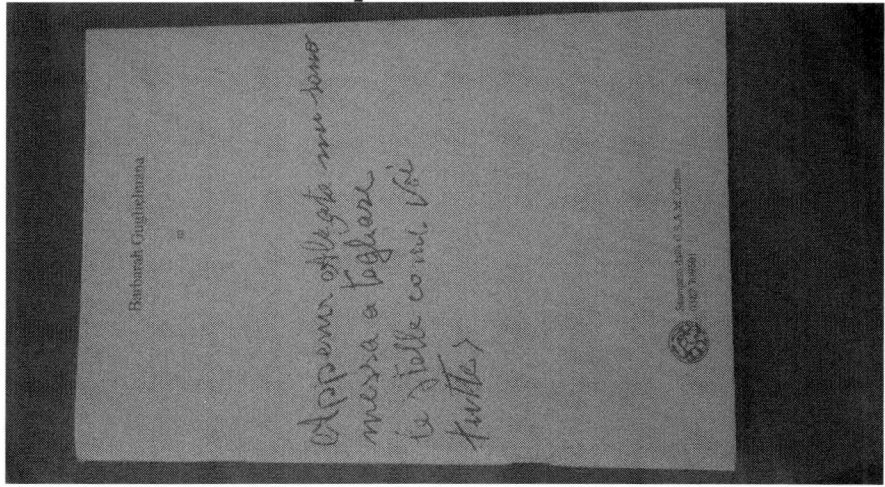

(The surprise gift)

185

GREECE

Part One: The Scammer

Whenever I visit Greece, I always have a crazy time. In fact, some of the weirdest things I have ever experienced happened there. I really like the country, the people are friendly and the history is mind-boggling.

I arrived in Athens for the first time around the 20th of February 2013, flying in from Rome. I was very thankful that they had a train that went directly into the city centre. I was extremely tired at this point in my travels, having lost around seven kilos. I was beginning to doubt if I was going to make it for the last two months of my trip. So, the little things like a simple train ride can make all the difference.

Dropping my bag off at the hostel (the creatively named "Athens Backpackers"), I walked out to see the Acropolis shining clearly in the background, above all the other buildings. It was a five-minute walk away, something which still seemed like a rather large distance in my current state of health.

One of the first things about the city that I noticed, was the large amounts of stray dogs in Athens. What I found particularly weird though, was that they were rather clean. In fact, they all looked well fed. As I walked through the streets, I noticed that the dogs seemed to have certain shops that they would go to for food. It was almost as if they were community dogs. It certainly explained why they were so well kept and friendly.

I eventually arrived at the Acropolis. The hill and the surrounding ruins were closed when I got there. I had to compromise and found that there was a small rocky hill nearby that I could climb up and check out the view below. I wasn't sure what type of rock it was, but it appeared similar to some sort of quartz or marble. It was very slippery to walk on. I guess many people over the years had used this vantage point to get a glimpse of all that was happening within.

Excited that I would be exploring this ancient place the next day, I decided that I would take a photo of myself. A "self shot" as the kids call it. I set the timer on my camera and took the image. Don't judge me, travelling alone means getting creative with photos. Selfie sticks were not yet the plague that they are today.

It was at this point, that I met an old man. More specifically, he met me. He had those sports style glasses that reflect so you can't see his eyes properly, short curly grey hair that was receding a little bit and, from an estimate, was about a hundred and sixty centimetres tall. Sorry, I didn't have a measuring tape with me, so you will have to deal with inaccurate details.

My point is, he did not have the appearance of an intimidating guy. He simply said "Hello" and asked, "Could you help me take a picture of me with the Acropolis in the background?" If you don't know already, Australians generally pride themselves on helping out people when they can and this guy seemed genuine. So, I obliged.

After I took the photo, I expected/hoped he would go on his way. But, he didn't disappear. To stop the awkwardness, I struck up a conversation. I didn't really ask for his life story. However, he seemed to be super determined to give it to me. He started explaining that he was doing this trip because his wife died. It was always their plan that they would explore Greece together. Now that she was gone, he was going to see all the places that they would have visited together. It was then, at the height of this heartbreaking story, that he asked if he could hang out with me while I walked and admired the historic location. How could I say no?

So we walked around, had a look at the wildlife (there are tortoises that live at the bottom of the Acropolis) and maintained a polite conversation. At some point he turned to me and said "I like you, you have been so kind to me, I want to buy you an ouzo to say thank you." I don't normally drink, but the guy seemed so earnest that I didn't really have an option for refusal. So, to my disappointment, we started to leave. I suggested a bar or two near to the Acropolis. "What about this one? It looks nice." He shook his head and said, "I saw one close to my hotel that I desperately want to try."

We got about halfway there, and then suddenly, I got a weird feeling. I'm not sure if it was the continued awkward conversation, or the weird determination to pass a series of perfectly fine-looking bars that got to me, yet, something was up. Trusting my gut, although feeling slightly bad for it, I decided to leave the gentleman to his trip. I made an excuse that I had promised my mother a photo of the Acropolis at sunset. I should head back to catch it. I thanked him for his company and tried to leave. He was quite disappointed and was rather insistent that I should come along. I distinctly recall him saying, "The weather would be clear tomorrow. You could get a better photo then." After some polite discussion, I managed to slip away.

The rest of my afternoon was lovely. I had a good time, seeing many of the locations I had been dreaming about for years. I walked through a bit of the neighbourhood and arrived back at the hostel. About five minutes later, someone new entered the room. He was a young man, tall and wearing loose clothing. A fuzzy beard adorned his face, a typical feature of long-term male travellers.

He was very, very upset. With lots of swearing and other expletives, the man began to tell a familiar story. It was of a little old Italian man that had lost his wife. I asked, "Did you meet him at the Acropolis?"

Through gritted teeth, he replied, "Yes." My heart was pounding. After a short pause to regain his composure, he con-

The Other Side Of Travelling

tinued. "The Italian wanted to take me to a bar. I thought the old guy could use some company and so, decided to go for one drink." Once he started talking in full sentences, his Australian accent came through loud and clear. More interesting for me though, was that he was telling me the exact same story that I had just gone through.

He continued to explain that they arrived at the suggested bar and sat down. It was empty, aside from them, the bartender and the waitress. In my head, I was spinning. What did I just avoid? The story continued.

Before long, the bartender asked, "Is it OK if I sit at the table with you? With so few customers, it would be easier to serve you both." The waitress sat down too and started looking with keen interest at our Australian friend. Finally, it seems, the waitress worked up the courage and asked him, "Want to buy me a drink?" Our Australian traveller was short of cash, but had already had a few drinks and as it was his last day in Europe, he thought, "Why not?" It was at this point that the scenario became extremely dodgy.

The bartender explained that he would have to pay up for the other drinks first. The Italian had offered to pay on the way there. However, it seems that, in his old age, he had now completely forgotten this offer. In fact, he seemed to not even hear the conversation taking place. He looked out into the distance, as if distracted by a memory. Trying to neutralise the situation, the Australian simply agreed to pay and asked for the bill. The bartender slid over the piece of paper. It was eighty euros. For three shots of Ouzo. If you haven't worked it out yet, this guy was about to get scammed.

Before he could get him out of this precarious situation, the security guard swiftly appeared behind him, blocking his exit. Our fellow traveller was now in a bar with no one that he knew and a bunch of people that wanted his money. The lead scammer/terrible bartender decided that now was the time to have a rational talk about their options. Man to man.

He politely explained, that, "You are getting screwed. You

are not leaving without paying the eighty euros. I feel sorry about this situation, but that is the way it is." If that wasn't enough, the bartender continued, "However, seeing as you are already getting metaphorically screwed for eighty euros, you might like to consider getting properly screwed for only forty euros more?" It was at this point, that he motioned to the waitress. She smiled again and winked.

As I was not there, I can't verify, but, he told me he paid the eighty euros and left. In my head, I was glad that I trusted my gut instinct, although I was a bit worried that it had taken that long to kick in. In a twist of fate, I actually saw the old Italian guy the next day at the Temple of Zeus and Hadrian's Arch. I even came back to Athens two years later and saw him again. So, either he is a scammer, or, I guess the guy was on a very long trip.

But, you want to know what the most annoying part is? The scammer was right. The weather was better the next day.

Part Two: The Dogs

The rest of my time in Athens was much more pleasant. As I continued my way through Greece, the good times continued. The archaeological sites made me drool, yet, something strange kept happening. It started in Athens, pretty much the day that I arrived and continued on my whole journey. Dogs. I mentioned them briefly before, but in order to tell this story I must make a disclaimer.

What I am about to say sounds unbelievable. At the very least it sounds like I took twelve tabs of LSD and ran naked around the town, screaming that the ancient ones were coming. However, I did not take LSD or any other drug and I swear that this story is true. I have never done marijuana in my life and my limited drinking career mostly ended once I was legally allowed to drink it (it just doesn't have the same appeal once you are allowed to do it). With this in mind, let us proceed.

The Other Side Of Travelling

It started in Athens, I woke up in the morning after my first night and there was a dog out the front of the hostel. It was a lean, short-haired dog with dark blonde hair. It looked a little like a mix between a greyhound and some other random breed that I couldn't pinpoint. I had seen it walking around the previous day and was surprised to see it there at the hostel. I figured that the owner of the hostel probably looked after the dog. I got my breakfast and ate it out the front. The dog sat nearby. I started to leave. The dog followed.

I went around the city with a Finnish man, named Janus. He was rocking white blonde dreadlocks and I had befriended him in the hostel. The dog still followed. It would bark at anyone that got close to us. Every place we went, it came with us. It followed us back to the hostel and was there the next day too.

Janus and I decided that we would check out Delphi and so walked to a taxi rank early one morning. We would take the taxi to the bus station and then, a three hour bus ride to get to the famous valley of oracles. The dog followed us to the taxi rank too. While strange, I assumed that it was the hostel's dog and perhaps hanged around with whoever it thought it would get food from. It did look really bummed out when it couldn't get in the taxi with us.

After a three hour bus ride through various scenic views and winding mountain roads, we arrived at Delphi. Stepping off the bus, there was a stray dog at the bus stop. This one was small with black hair and it looked almost like it had a beard. Its tail was short. I took a look around at the beautiful valley before me and began to understand why you might choose this as a place for your oracles. From there, we started to head off. The dog followed us, or more precisely, I guess we followed it. It was slightly in front and waited for us. It actually guided us to the entrance where they were selling tickets to visit the ruins of the Oracle of Delphi. I was starting to get freaked out at this point. The dog knew where we wanted to go. I was also thinking of changing my name to the Dog Whisperer because I clearly had a talent that I was unaware of. This dog followed us around Delphi all day.

About halfway through our trip to Delphi, as we were walking from where the majority of the temples were, to a small section removed from the rest, I looked down at the valley from the road. There, I saw something that I had never seen before in my life. It seemed like before my very eyes, a cloud was forming below us in the valley. As it rose, it grew bigger and bigger. By the time it hit our level, it had basically engulfed and drenched us to the bone. It rose higher and just as quickly as it had arrived, it was gone. In fact, after that, it was perfectly sunny. Five minutes of rain and back to nice, comfortable Mediterranean weather. It was a weird experience and the look of that cloud rolling and swelling as it moved towards us is not be one that I will forget for a long time.

We went back to Athens with the bus after we had seen everything. The hostel dog was waiting there. The next morning, upon the recommendation of the hostel bartender, we got up really early and went to Meteora. For those that don't know, I am not referring to the second album from the rock band Linkin Park. It is actually a famous area where some orthodox monks live. For those who don't know who Linkin Park is, they were a hard rock band that was famous in the early 2000s. For those of you that don't know what hard rock is, imagine Elvis, with heavy electric guitars, faster drums and a lot of screaming.

Anyway, before tourists came, the monks would haul themselves up with rope elevators hundreds of meters high. That is epic. Now, they have a bridge. I prefer this option. I am a short man and figure I was meant to stay close to the ground. I think I would have made many messes from many places if I had to take a rope elevator.

When we arrived in Meteora, there is only one thing to do, hike the mountain to see the monks. We headed towards the base, leaving the village behind. We were looking at the epic mountain range before us. It was such a weird formation, with the mountains looking like they had been rounded off. It didn't have that "sharp" look of some other mountains. I hope you understand what I mean.

At the base of the mountain, we found a dog. It was a sheep-dog-like breed, it was very dirty and it barked at us. With the dirt and everything, it looked almost like it was one step away from dreadlocks. Given the past few days' experiences, I resisted the temptation to bark back.

It was blocking our path to the mountain pass so I called it Leonidas after the famous Spartan King that gym junkies everywhere idolise. As we approached, it started to walk up the path, leading us. At this point, I assume that I have lost half my readers, but seriously, the dog led us up the mountain. In fact, it even stopped for photo ops. It led us off the path. By now, I was willing to follow a street dog into a dangerous unknown wilderness and was pleasantly surprised to find him sitting on the edge of a rock with the view of the mountains behind. He sat and waited for me and Janus to take our photos. Like any good tour guide, it let us know that we had to keep moving, barked at us, and led us back to the path. We continued up the mountain and eventually reached the monastery.

The dog waited patiently outside (they weren't allowed in) while we checked out the place. The monastery was clean, with a good view. Honestly though, I don't think I could live there. There were very few monks around to talk to. I guess they were busy, but we did meet one or two. There were also a few human skulls around. I guess that is the ultimate honour. If you have been a good monk, then you get to be part of the monastery on a permanent basis.

When we left the building a good half an hour later, the dog was still there, waiting patiently like a shaggy sentinel. He barked at us as if to say 'Let's go'. Leonidas led us back down the mountain. I was having so much fun. We got back down to the base and then he disappeared. He just left us. We heard one last bark and he was gone.

Janus and I woke up the next morning to try to explore the other monasteries. To my disappointment, Leonidas was not there, but another dog guided us up a different path. I like to think that Leonidas was busy, so he sent a colleague. This dog had short straw-coloured hair with an almost white belly. On the way up, it took us to a cave before showing us to the monasteries in the area.

The cave was pretty interesting. We had a great time exploring it. At some point, a decent way into the cave, we saw that there was a drop. We climbed down and looked up. It was then that we realised that the floor that we had just been exploring was nothing more than fallen rocks, sticks and dust piled on one another. It was thick and probably very stable. Nonetheless, I immediately started to see images in my head of a series of collapses trapping me in there forever. The whole way back out of the cave I did not quite feel as safe or as confident as I had going in. Pictures of me falling into dark cavernous ravines with no one to save me continued to fill my brain long after we left.

However, before I exited, I was still stupid enough to climb up the wall to get a glimpse through a hole in the roof of the cave. On my way back down, I slipped. Luckily, my arms were locked in at the time, stopping me from falling. Unluckily, the position I was in created a pivot point to which the weight of the rest of my body swung. My legs slammed right into the roof of the cave. It didn't hurt. However, it was enough for me to say, that I should move on from this place.

It was only when I got out of the cave that I realised there was a giant hole in my left boot where one shouldn't have been. I think that when my legs swung, they must have hit a spike in the roof or something. The quality of my boots were questionable and I was lucky to escape injury that time. I had a look online later and found out that the whole area is riddled with caves, which were used for various purposes. One is even mentioned as having been the lair of a dragon. If I ever go back, I would like to have a look at these other caves and go exploring.

After leaving the cave, we eventually made it to the top and explored some of the other monasteries. They all provided spectacular views. It was a great trip and well worth it. Leonidas' colleague left as we entered the first monastery. Clearly, the work ethic was not as strong in this one.

As a side note, on the way back down to the train station, a man on a moped stopped us. He was clearly drunk. His driving gave it away, but as he came closer, the smell gave us the secondary evidence to make a satisfactory conclusion. He pulled out a flyer and told us we should stay at his hotel. We explained we were leaving today and had already paid for the hotel we had stayed at. Yet, he would not take no for an answer. Shoving the flyer into our hands, he was off. Looking at the photo of the view from the hotel, we realised that it was not geographically possible. The owner (perhaps our moped-driving hype man) had photo-shopped the mountains of Meteora behind his café view. The way it was all presented would just not work. I kept the flyer because if I go back there, I want to stay there just to see the guy again.

On my other trips to Greece, there were always more dogs. However, these are the best stories. I have gotten used to the weird looks I get when I tell these stories. I try to think that you are all just jealous that you don't have cool dog stories from Greece. It's not me, it's you...right?

The Bees

About two years after my trip with Leonidas, I went back to Greece. Heidi, who you may remember from my trip to Cairns, came along too. My goal this time was Mycenae to see the Lion Gate and Agamemnon's Tomb. Everyone knows it is not really his tomb, but Schliemann, the full-time demolition man and part-time archaeologist, decided that it would be better for publicity's sake if that is what it was. He even had his wife pose with the jewels and sent it to the press. Even still, it is quite well preserved and well worth the visit if you have the time.

Getting there involved making our way to the Athens main bus station. I mentioned it in a previous story, yet, it deserves a small description. Dirty, with no clear signing for English speakers, it is a tough place to navigate and understand. If you can work it out though, there are many places that one can get to, for a relatively cheap price. Just go to the toilets somewhere else before you arrive. You will thank me later for that one.

The city of Mycenae, found near the modern day Mykines, is positioned on a hill, a perfect defensive position. In modern times, there are lots of orange farms around the area and there are eucalyptus trees lining parts of the streets leading to the ancient town. When you finally arrive, you have a number of choices, but the most common is to head to the main gate to the city. The Lion Gate, as it is called, was amazing. I was living out a childhood dream. I stared at that thing for ages, just trying to imagine all the craziness it went through. However, while that was exciting, I really started to have fun in the well.

The well was like a miniature mine with steps leading down to the water table. It was located right in the far back corner of the archaeological site. There was no light and you could only go in so far. After a certain point, it was blocked with a velvet rope. Those velvet ropes always have soooo much power. Heidi was off taking photos of some awesome lizards she had found. I wanted to explore.

I was at the entrance when I noticed that a girl next to me was looking into the darkness with apprehension. I asked her, "Are you feeling OK?" She said, "I'm fine, but I'm not sure if I should go down there." There was no clear signage to say that we were not allowed to enter that part. I know I shouldn't have done it, but my mischievous side took over. I turned to the girl and said, "I'll go down first and call back if it was clear to come down."

Proceeding into the cave, once out of sight, I started

screaming and then ran back out. She took flight. Not my finest hour, yet, I just couldn't resist. I hope that I can learn to be less annoying, but even at twenty nine, I still find this immature stuff amusing. Heidi, having now found other interesting animals to look at, only heard the girl screaming. When I returned, Heidi asked, "What was all that about?" I shrugged and moved on.

After a while it came to the main event, the big reason for the trip out to the town. I went to the tombs.

The tombs are called tholos tombs (otherwise known as beehive tombs) because of their shape. I visited four or five in various degrees of preservation that were just below the main entrance to the citadel. The main one was some distance away from the rest of the preserved city. However, when I got to the big one, Mr Agamemnon's, the security guard stopped me. I was not in the mood. I was hyped to see the tomb. I was also warm and impatient. She said, "No one is to enter this tomb today." I asked her why, as calmly as possible. She proceeded to explain, "There are bees inside." How ironic. A bee infestation in a tholos tomb.

Regardless, I was determined. I begged, "Can I walk and take a photo of the hundred metre lead up to the entrance? She gave her approval. So, taking my camera and being as ready as possible to run in and out if the opportunity came to get a glimpse, I rounded the corner. Heidi followed hesitantly behind me.

It was then that the sound hit us. It was like a beehive was next to a Marshall amp and mic set up. The noise from the colony was so loud, I couldn't even believe it.

Was this a practical joke? I looked around for the cameras, capturing on film the silly tourist (me) falling for the trap. It seems that the beehive tomb was completely infested. The shape probably also amplified the sound. I didn't run in. While disappointed that I couldn't go in, you can't say that the Greeks didn't warn us. I mean, it is right in there with the name.

We left the area and headed back to the bus stop. Along the way we tasted some of the oranges in the farms. They were really nice. When the bus arrived, Heidi and I hopped on and we were back into Athens before we knew it. That evening, we looked in the mirror and saw how sunburned we both were. It was fifteen degrees out there and we still got our arses kicked by the sun. Heidi, being a redhead got the worst of it. Still, it healed pretty quickly, over the next few days. Don't forget your sunscreen.

The Sand Storm

After this, Heidi and I flew into Crete. To be honest, until we landed, I wasn't sure we were going to make it. The runway runs parallel to the shore. A strong wind was blowing in from the north and as the pilot lined the plane up with the runway, the strong gusts kept tilting the plane sharply to its right side. As we got closer to land, these movements gave me more and more fear that the next gust would blow the right wing into the ground and we would all burst into flames.

While I was hyperventilating, Heidi was reading her magazine. The pilot managed to land and the whole plane clapped with joy. I could hear the united sigh of relief as the plane became stable on the tarmac. Heidi calmly placed her magazine in her rucksack and we left the plane.

After we arrived at the hotel and dropped our equipment off, Heidi and I had a quick walk around the city to get our orientation. My main goal in this area and a life long dream was to visit the Knossos castle. The next day would be the day to fulfil that dream.

We arrived early to the compound, but not early enough. There were school groups everywhere. Little kids were running in circles, too young to fully get a grip on the epicness that lay before them. Even still, as they were on guided tours, we managed to get around and see most of the castle without disruption.

The Other Side Of Travelling

I must say I was a little let down. I had built it up too much in my head. There has been a lot of restoration at Knossos, with a lot of imagination used to fill the gaps. While this makes it more impressive at first sight, it is not very original. It could very likely be entirely wrong. If I wanted an interpretation, I could do that myself. I would have preferred the unaltered ruins and use the information to build my own picture. However, we can't have everything. Heidi, with no such preconceptions about the location was very happily examining the buildings and taking photos of the unique surroundings.

Over the course of the visit, the wind picked up again, until it was almost gale force. I looked out towards the valley behind the castle and could see a red tinge in the air coming towards us. The longer I stared, the thicker the cloud of red became.

A sandstorm was coming in from Africa. They started to move us out of the area for safety reasons. This is when I saw one of the most interesting examples of a wind tunnel in my life. As visibility began to dwindle and the little children in the school group followed their teacher calmly out of the building in single file, they had to cross a break in one of the walls surrounding the main courtyard. Here, the wind forces were all concentrated. The adults passed through fine, and only their finely styled hair was slightly ruffled. What happened next though was amazing.

One after another, the kids walked past this gap. As soon as they hit it, the wind got caught in their yellow high visibility vests. The vest blew up like a balloon and, "whoosh!", they went flying. The amazing part was that the next kid, seeing their friend flying off, did not hesitate, but followed suit.

Child after child battled that wind tunnel and lost, until about three or four of them were on the ground tumbling across an ancient royal courtyard like a bunch of neon yellow tumble-weeds. Finally, the teacher stopped and gathered the little ones. They were OK. Perhaps, a little dizzy. One or two seemed as if they wanted to go for a second round.

Sometimes the people are the best bit

I didn't see as much of Crete as I would have liked, given that I was only there a short time. However, I did get the opportunity to interact with the people living on the beautiful island. They are amazing. If you ever get the chance, go before the tourist season. I recommend March. Find a local restaurant and just check out the whole place. The amount of food being placed on the table is unnerving. The battles over who has the honour to pay are epic struggles of dominance. Everyone wants to pay for everyone. They can't eat all the food on the table, which seems to please the waiter. To reward their patrons with their overfull stomachs, they bring out Raki, in addition to fruit and fried doughnuts. Just think about it, they were so full that half of the food on the table was left uneaten, and the reward is more food.

A quick note. Cretan Raki is different from Turkish Raki or ouzo. Closer to a Grappa, but don't let a Cretan hear you say that, or you might not make it back off the island.

I had a problem even to pay the waiter. Heidi and I had ordered some food before we saw what the portion sizes were. When the plates landed on our table, we discovered that we had ordered way too much. I had ordered a small bottle of raki to test it. When the waiter came to pick the food up, he brought back the dessert as described. We hadn't even finished the first bottle of raki but as I went to pay it seemed like I wasn't allowed. I would pull the cash out, the waiter would examine the bottle of raki, decide that my partner in crime and I had not had enough yet, pour a new shot into each glass and then walk away. It took me at least four shots before I could pay for everything. I slept well that night.

As I said, in general the people were very relaxed. It was very nice to see. Even on the roads they are relaxed. In fact, they are still getting used to the concept of a dual carriageway. On one particularly sunny day, we saw an old man, on a moped, going about thirty kilometres an hour down the highway. It has a speed limit of a hundred kilometre per hour. He was on the phone and people were honking. He was using both of the lanes at the same time, plus the side strip for his travels. When someone finally passed, he managed, while still on the phone, to lift the other hand up, give the finger and then continue swerving from side to side. I recommend taking the bus if you want to travel without too much stress on the main roads.

The hills are not much better for driving, with wild goats and other animals often blocking the path and generally causing various degrees of annoyance and danger to the driver. I wanted to find some ancient ruins on a mountain peak. Heidi, with more experience driving on the right-hand side of the road, was at the wheel, while I was the navigator. We found only a herd of goats blocking our path. We had to turn back at some point and admit defeat. Nature may be on the ropes, but will still find a way to cause problems when it can. I'm glad it was goats and not roadworks.

Pigeons of Doom

I have to say that I did have one problem in Crete. Getting information. In general, the stories and locations are so old that various myths and theories pop up to explain what happened and where. This makes getting a straight answer about anything difficult.

For example, we heard of a cave in the mountains on the north-eastern coastline that was said to be the inspiration for the legend of the Minotaur and the Labyrinth. Heidi and I drove up to the location through many hills. The roads seemed to not be clearly labelled and there was a general remoteness that somehow exuded creepiness. We parked the car near a church and made our way down through the entrance into a cave. It had a wide gaping entrance and looked like it would swallow anyone up and take them straight down to Hades.

Still, interest gripped me and I made my way down. I soon found that my torch was nowhere near strong enough to penetrate the darkness and general gloom that was there in that damp cave.

I walked around and saw what I could. It was interesting, but the whole time that I was there, an eerie sound followed me. After some investigation, I discovered that there was a bunch of pigeons in the cave. The cooing of the birds in the cave created an echo effect that was spine chilling. I never thought the flying rats could be scary for anything other than rabies. Either way, we eventually left the cave.

When we looked up the cave in more detail later, there was a suggestion that human sacrifice may have taken place there. So, maybe it wasn't the pigeons after all giving me the goosebumps.

Zeus's birthplaces

My final recommendation, if you go to Crete, is to check out Zeus' birthplace. Be warned though. It is another example of this conflicting information that is difficult to follow.

There are two locations for the birth of Zeus, with one located on the east side of the island and the other located on the west side. I guess the idea is to visit both if you can and decide which is the most kingly and such. However, it would make my life a lot easier if they could decide on which one was which. Either way, the one on the east side is where I visited.

It was amazing. The drive up there was picturesque, going through winding roads into the mountains. We were only stopped by a few goats this time. At quite a height, things level off and there seems to be a valley within the peak of the mountain. Driving around, and then up the final part of the mountain, you reach the car park. After that, you still have to walk up a steep section of the mountain. When you finally get to the cave entrance, you take a series of stairs down a steep descent.

The lights they have chosen give all the walls a green tinge to them. I don't know why they chose the colour. Maybe it's for the wildlife or something. Whatever the reason, the pools and water flowing in the cave, along with the lights, gives it a unique atmosphere. I don't know if that was a place I would want the king of my gods to have been born and raised. But, who am I to judge? It was a cool place to visit all the same. Well worth the trip.

If I get the chance to go back to Greece (and I really hope I do), I will check out the western part of the island of Crete. There is a canyon there that I want to hike through. I would also like to see Mount Olympus on the mainland of Greece and see where the Olympic games first started. Maybe find some more dogs. Get your bag packed and go.

Daniel Greenwood

(Photo taken right before scammer came to say "Hi")

(Athens dog)

The Other Side Of Travelling

(Cloud forming in Delphi)

(The mighty Leonidas)

Daniel Greenwood

(Cave in Meteora)

(One of the monasteries)

The Other Side Of Travelling

(Agamemnon's tomb)

(Knossos Castle, before the sand storm came)

207

Daniel Greenwood

(Potential birthplace of Zeus)

AUSTRIA

You want to meet there?

Vienna and I did not get along. I arrived there shortly after my visit to Meteora with Janus and Leonidas. I was tired, poor and sick. Vienna was expensive. I walked around the city, went to the top of a church for a view of the city. It was OK, but ultimately, I only had three days there and not a lot of cash, so finding things to my taste was difficult. I did try and even spent a ridiculous amount of euros for entry to a museum. I came to Vienna from Greece, where museums are cheap and the artefacts are plenty. In Vienna, I paid three times what I paid to enter the Acropolis and had nowhere near as much to check out. I even found out later that the provenance of the major piece, an Aztec headdress, is disputed. So I felt that my money was a bit wasted there.

Rather annoyed and frustrated, I returned to the hostel. There, I bumped into a few Polish gentlemen on a little trip. One guy's name was Marcin and he was there with some of his friends. They invited me to hang out with them, which was cool. Throughout the day we chilled and played table tennis in the hostel. Then Marcin invited me up to their room for a drink.

I don't normally drink, but explained that I would come up to keep the conversation going. I didn't understand that not drinking was not an option. They offered me a glass of vodka. Before I even had the chance to say no, they had gone to the window, opened it up and taken a huge bottle out from the snow laying on the window sill. Perhaps slightly irresponsible as, if the snow got dislodged, a very heavy bottle would join it on its journey to the ground. On the other hand, it definitely kept the drink at the right temperature.

I didn't want to be rude, so I took the drink, shot it as best I could and tried not to pull a face as if I had just drunk a litre of gasoline. It was better than most other vodka that I had tried. It had a raspberry flavour to it which was nice. Even more important, it actually tasted like raspberry. Often those flavoured vodkas taste nothing like they are claiming to be. I guess I passed my test with the shot, so the night continued.

I am not sure why, but eventually Marcin and the boys decided they wanted to check out a cemetery. I can't say if the drinks had anything to do with it. I, clearly making well thought out decisions, decided to join. There was nothing strange about going to a cemetery with four Polish men you have just met, in a town you don't know. You don't do that every weekend? No? So, just me?

Yeah, looking back at it, the idea was a bit dodgy. In the end, it didn't matter. The cemetery was closed on the account of it being 8 pm and a very odd time to go visit. The Polish guys decided that at the least, a selfie should be taken to commemorate our adventure. It turned out OK. I still have it in one of my photo albums. I said good night after that and went back to the hostel. I know, not even a little devil worship or something before bed, but what could I say, the place just wasn't open. Not like we could have jumped the fence or something.

I left Vienna the next day for Prague. My wallet was glad for the change of city.

The Other Side Of Travelling

(The entrance to the cemetery)

(Vienna)

CZECH REPUBLIC

A Museum with a different experience

Prague is an extremely beautiful city. It is also very popular with tourists. It is possible, if you move at a reasonable pace, to easily walk from all the major sites and see everything in a day or two without missing all too much. This makes it easy for all sorts of people to come, get a taste and leave on a tight schedule. When you move so quickly through a city though, you often miss out on some of the finer details.

Let me give you an example. If you visit Prague, there are two museums based on the communist times of the Czech Republic. The first, better known example is the Communist Museum. It has reasonable displays. However, when I visited it, I got the feeling that it is reasonably old. It could really do with an update. The other one that I visited was the KGB museum. This place is crazy and, if you get the chance, you must go. Though be prepared, the museum is, shall we say, um, unconventional.

Upon entrance, you cannot see much, just the front counter. Your view to the right is blocked by a sort of temporary wall. Often, there is no one there. If you wait long enough, a man with a sort of buzz cut will arrive to sell you your ticket. You enter the building. The ticket man takes a step to the left (your right) and now explains he is the tour guide.

When I arrived, it was obvious he was already on a tour, but he started it again from scratch for me, whether the others liked it or not. I can still see the faces of the others looking at me, half frustrated that I arrived and also with a sort of warn-

The Other Side Of Travelling

ing look, that seemed to say "get out while you still can." I figured they were afraid of learning something new, so smiled and took my place in the group.

He started by explaining that, "My English is not so good and to please be patient." My Russian and Czech are non-existent, and coming from Australia, many people from England would debate if we even speak English. So, I couldn't complain. I was just excited to pull out whatever information I could. He began to go through the whole founding of the KGB. He enthusiastically talked about the KGB issue cocaine dispenser, for when vodka was not allowed. It looked like a giant scorpion. While I was looking at the scorpion with a removable back to store powder, I heard noises behind me. When I turn back, I see the guy has pulled out a gun.

I could see it, it was shining. The light was hitting it at just the right angle. I could see where the bullet would come down and blow my brains to bits if it was pointed at me. He gave me the gun. I looked at it, then at him, then the rest of the people in the group. He looked very confused, as if I had missed some major point. After a short pause, staring intensely at me he says "Where is camera? Why you not take photos?"

I, still half terrified, oblige. But, from the look of his face, I could tell that I was still doing something wrong. I don't know why, but he still seemed unimpressed, annoyed even. In a moment, he decided what was missing. He gave me a hat, aviator style glasses and pulled out a tactical knife, which he gave to me. "That's better." I was now allowed to proceed taking photos.

Eventually my tour guide decides that there is enough photos. BUT ONLY WITH THAT GUN. He takes away the tactical knife and replaces it with a different sort of pistol. I can't see where he is pulling all these weapons from. He seems like one of those computer game characters which appear to be able to carry twenty weapons and still move like they are only in their birthday suit. Now that I have two guns, I am again made to do an impromptu photo shoot, but I had to be careful not to hit the guns on one another because, as he explained to me, "I have just cleaned them."

After that, the pistols were taken away. I had two seconds to recover before they were replaced with a sub machine gun of sorts, with a shoulder strap. This one, at least, I saw him take from the wall. All in all, a curious start to tour.

The rest of the tour was over pretty quickly. The museum was actually just a room with stuff the owner had collected over the years. I can't be too sure, however, I think some might have made their way to the museum shortly after the wall broke down. In his basement, he had a plaster caste of Lenin's face and a picture of Putin hung proudly in pride of place in the centre of the wall. As I said, unconventional, but interactive.

It was so good, in fact, that when I met an American Navy guy on a walking tour later that day, by the name of Joey, I took him back there. We had to escape from the snow anyway. While the snow was charming, this was a far more interesting experience for me. I still catch Joey around every now and again and we always have a good laugh about that place.

Anyway, as we left, we passed the American Embassy, where they were checking for bombs using mirrors under each of the cars that passed through the street. To go from one intense scene (in historical terms) to seeing how suspicious the American Embassy was of all passing cars shows that those times of craziness are perhaps not as over as they first appeared.

Aside from that, the other thing I recommend seeing in Prague is the Big Metal Babies. I still to this day don't know what they are there for, but if you take a detour to a small park near the Palace side of Charles Bridge, along with the Lennon wall (yes that Lennon) there are three giant, black, metal babies with bar codes for faces. The few people that found them struck creative poses. Some climbed on the babies. Others crawled with the babies.

It is the first piece of modern art that I actually didn't

mind. The art work itself is up to your interpretation, but I think it's pretty clear what the message is. There are supposedly a few more of these babies around, though I am yet to find them. I heard some were climbing up one of the TV towers like an invasion of the metal babies. Whatever they are there for, it brings an interesting contrast to the old buildings throughout the city.

Promoting with Style

I went back to Prague a few years after my first visit. This time my best mate, Andy, came along for the ride. I had known Andy since high school. Andy was a tall, well-built man, with very light brown/dark blonde hair. He had come to visit me in Europe at the end of his service in the army.

I had already seen many of the things in Prague that I wanted to. Yet sometimes, by going back you can gain new perspective. When I was there last, it was winter. Now it was the middle of August, hot and full of tourists.

As is standard with every visit to Prague, I went to visit the clock. The clock itself has a controversial history. It is not a happy clock. It is constantly reminding people that death is near and that they will either go to heaven or hell one day. It shows the twelve apostles, as leading role models. It also shows some stereotypical sinners who all shake their head as the skeleton rings the bell. Rather intense thing to walk past every morning.

Last time, I had it really easy and would pass it a couple of times a day, just to see it go off. However, this time, I had to fight my way through hundreds of people to get a glimpse. As my friend and I had finally found our positions, over to the right of the clock, I saw the crowd part.

It seemed like a sort of parade was taking place. There were around five or so musicians and they were dressed in old fashion clothes. They were marching in single file, making a path through the masses waiting for the clock to do its thing.

At first, I figured that this was part of a performance put on for the summer. But the last guy, with much gusto and bravado, was holding pamphlets. In a windmill wide action, he was handing out advertisement to everyone. Normally, when I see people handing out pamphlets, they either get ignored or you see the paper thrown on the ground a metre or two away from the promoter. This was not the case this time.

The people seemed to be in such a state of shock that, as the paper landed in the hand of the unsuspecting tourist, they simply took it and smiled. No abuse or anything. Maybe it was just that the crowds were so big that there was no escape anyway. It was an interesting way to make an entrance.

Conflicting Orders

Andy and I also went to the Golden Mile of the Palace. I didn't have the cash to do that last time, so it was something new to me. There are lots of little activities to do there. I had a go at shooting a crossbow. It's harder than you might think. However, I managed to do OK and don't think I missed the target entirely. I am no sharpshooter though. Otherwise it was basic ye olde stuff. Fun, but pretty standard.

We left the mile and were looking to check out a different part of the palace. Andy and I very quickly got lost. I can only assume that we took a wrong turn somewhere. We ended up in another paid area of the castle. This was a major problem, as we hadn't paid for said area. We decided that the only thing to do was to back track. We failed even to do that. It was hot, we were tired and not thinking clearly. The two of us got even more lost.

Finally, Andy found a way out to the paid area. It was not what you would call "the official" entrance. It involved jumping a small fence. We looked around and could see no other way around it without wasting hours back in the maze we had just come from. The sun was blazing and we just wanted to find a good place to sit. It seemed as if the coast was clear of po-

The Other Side Of Travelling

lice and security.

As quickly and as carefully as we could, I scrambled over the fence and then Andy, being far more sporty than I, followed with a casual leap over the fence. No sooner had we four feet in the free area of the castle, when two tall men with three day growth stopped us.

"Go back," they said. We were very confused. We had clearly not taken a normal entrance. We were not intending to repeat that performance unnecessarily. It would also mean jumping the fence back into the paid area which we had no ticket for. They were insistent that we go back and showed badges. They were undercover police.

Andy and I were not sure of what to do, particularly, as to go backwards in front of the police was to break in, directly in front of the police. Generally, breaking rules in front of the cops is not a good idea. We had broken one by accident. The next one would be deliberate. To my luck, and restored faith in humanity, the gardener came up and started talking to the police. I don't know what he said, but he must have backed us up and we were reluctantly let go. However, we were warned that if we did anything like that again, we would be in a lot of trouble. I believed them entirely and was an absolute angel for the rest of the trip.

I did check out those babies again before I left. The ones with the bar codes. Still have no clue what the hell they are there for. I'm not sure that I ever will. Still fascinating though. Plus the Lennon wall, as always, had new graffiti, so that was interesting. A short trip, but a good one. The other communist museum has had an upgrade too. Looking very modern and fancy.

Daniel Greenwood

(One of the babies)

The Other Side Of Travelling

(The clock, before the promoters came)

(Lennon Wall)

Daniel Greenwood

(Armour on the Golden Mile)

(Change of Guard, Prague Castle)

GERMANY

Mississippi

Mr Moustache had a large moustache that could be twirled. I know it twirled because he kept twirling it. He also had slicked-back hair and wore stylish clothes. A grey vest, some nice black slacks. It was quite unusual gear for a traveller.

I met him, while in Munich, on one of those free walking tours found in a lot of European cities. They are not really free, the guides are working for tips. Yet they are labelled as free, because technically, you don't have to pay anything. (As a side note, if you do take one of these, often the tour guide must pay the company €2.50 per person they take. Consider paying them at least that so they break even). The quality of the tour varies, but the one I had just taken was relatively good. It was perhaps one of those rare occasions where you get more than you paid for. The guide knew her facts, was funny and entertaining and was actually able to answer questions, which showed that she had not just learned a script.

Given the subject matter, it did feel a bit awkward at times. For example, we were taken to the Hofbrauhaus. It has a lot of history. When you look up at the roof, you can see a bunch of flags set in a recurring pattern. Unfortunately, it takes all of about two seconds to realise what was truly underneath the paint. We were told by the guide that it was originally covered with swastikas. Now, it seems, it was brightly coloured swastika shaped flags floating above peoples heads as they ate their schnitzel and drunk their litre beers. For a country trying to move on from a terrible time, this was an example of a mark that they just could not erase. I looked up at it, impressed that the building had even survived. The others in the group looked equally shocked. Master Moustache twirled his bushy lip curtain with intrigue.

But it was not all bad. Down one particular street there were four lion statues. The nose of every one was rubbed shiny. The tale is that you can rub any three of the four and get the qualities in areas of life that the statues represent (love, money, health and luck). The problem is however, they don't tell you which ones are which and if you rub all four, then you are doomed to bad luck.

Of course, as a bunch of tourists, we went and debated the merits of each lion, to try and determine what it represented. As I debated which ones I would choose, I caught the Moustachioed Man out of the corner of my eye, walking up to the lion on the far left with an air of confidence. He had that twinkle in his eye that said, "I know something that you don't." The rest of the group and I picked our three while the sharp dressed man waited, leaning against a wall, observing us intently. He just couldn't seem to keep his hands off that well-preened moustache.

Anyway, after the tour, as it was freezing cold and snowing, a few of us, including the magical Mr Moustache, decided to go to a bar to find out about how it was that everyone made it to Munich and what was their reason for being there. As we were in the heart of Bavaria, it also meant large amounts of German Beer.

Myself being unable to drink beer without vomiting from both ends profusely (both due to the taste and an unfortunate gluten allergy that I maintain I had before it was cool), I decided to have a nice, giant, manly glass of Cola.

My other companions were a motley crew. The most prominent was the aforementioned Mr Moustache. A young lady and gentleman from Canada came along too. The lady's name was Sarah and she seemed to me to be very sporty.

The Other Side Of Travelling

She had long brown hair and a fringe that kept getting in her eyes. The gentleman went by the name of Adam. His clothes seemed way too big for him and his eyes were full of energy. He was wearing his hat backwards and told me later that he wanted to be a comedian. A friendly chap from Ireland with a beard and shaggy hair joined us too. Finally, an American with a short clean haircut from a state that escapes me, completed the group. He looked like he might have been in the army before.

Mr Moustache was clear to point out early on, that he was from Mississippi. It was something that he really wanted to get across to us. It seemed to be very important to him. Adam and Sarah (the Canadians) nodded politely while the other American and the Irishman talked intently about their next destination. Over the next twenty minutes or so, while we were waiting for the very inefficient waiter to deliver our drinks, we discussed the tour and debated the highlights.

I am still not sure why, but, at some point a rivalry emerged between the Canadians and Mr Moustache Mississippi. Well, I say emerged, because as far as I could see, the only person out of all the participants in this feud, that was aware of the competition was Mr Moustache himself. The first beers arrived and our moustachioed crusader had a fire in his eyes. The bar was empty besides us, but Moustache Dude wanted to impress his audience, and immediately drank his whole half litre beer. Twirling his moustache and glaring at the Canadians, he waited for their move. While he waited, he ordered his second beer. Adam and Sarah on the other hand, totally unaware they were in a very serious drinking challenge for the honour of their country, continued to drink and enjoy their expensive beers quite slowly. They tried to make conversation with the guy, asking the normal travel questions. However, even though Mr Moustache would answer the questions, he seemed to be almost annoyed. All the conversation seemed to be getting in the way of his real goal.

As if to make it very clear that the Canadians were falling

behind, Mr Moustache drunk his second half litre as soon as it arrived and then explained that, "You are both falling behind."

To his utter confusion, they didn't understand what he meant. I think Sarah's exact word was, "Huh?" The Irishman and the other American were also confused. They looked at me briefly, both shrugged their shoulders and delved back into their conversation on whether it was better to travel in Autumn or Spring.

Monsieur Moustache came to the conclusion that, if he was going to beat these sneaky maple-syrup drinking Canadians, he was going to have to go big or go home. Over the course of the next hour or so, he drank another four half litre beers. Then proceeded to fall asleep. I guess drinking is tough work. It was a lot of beer. With Sarah and Adam finally realising that they had unwillingly been part of a drinking challenge, they proceeded to celebrate their surprise victory.

All around us, almost as soon as his immaculately-trimmed moustache hit the table (of course, still maintaining perfect form), the party began in earnest. Our conversation moved from the standard topics of a first meeting to more meaty subjects. As I said, Adam had dreams of being in show business. The Irishman simply wanted to travel for as long as he could possibly manage it. The army guy and Sarah were both there on short holidays and were dreading returning to their jobs.

As our conversation continued, two groups of football fans supporting rival teams had entered the bar and were chanting at one another. One was Bayern and I think the other was Dortmund. I am not sure though. I don't know soccer teams that well.

Slowly at first, but building with each round of chants and round of beers, eventually the fans were on the tables, slamming glasses on the benches and singing very loudly. Moustache Man, sensing that his input was needed and in a strange moment of composure, proceeded to try and sing, lifted his head and slapped his hands on the table a few times. He smiled his victorious smile at the still-confused Canadians and fell back to sleep. The whole contribution was no more than fifteen seconds.

Eventually, we all decided to head back to our respective hostels. It was still reasonably light. The tour had finished at 1 pm and we had only been in the bar a few hours. Dark was coming in though. We thought it was best to bring Master Moustache back with us. After much encouragement, and quite a lot of lifting, we managed to get him almost back to the district where he said his hostel was. He even seemed to come to himself a little bit and was able to almost stand on his own legs. We propped him against a wall so we could press the button to cross the road.

I am still unsure to this day exactly what happened, but at some point, between the time when we propped him up and pressing the button, he disappeared. Gone. *Verschwunden*, as the Germans would say. He just melted into the crowd of people around us. I never saw him again.

Sometimes I lie awake at night and wonder what this guy did after he left us. The most logical theory is that he went on to get more beer. Still, maybe it was something different. Was he taken back to the hostel? Was he frozen in the snow? Will the beautiful people of Munich step outside one day as the ice melts and trip on an immaculately-preserved moustache? Maybe he hibernated. He surely had enough alcohol in him to work as an antifreeze. Perhaps, still holding the grin of his one-sided victory, he will arise to challenge the next worthy, if unaware, opponent. Either way, I hope that he is OK and that he got to wherever he was headed safely. Sometimes in travel, the question is more interesting than the answer. I keep an eye out for him.

The Devil's Church

After that exciting adventure, the next place I visited in Munich was the Church where Pope Benedict served before he became the Pope. It is called the Frauenkirche. It goes by another name though. The Devil's Footprint Church. Now, hold off on your jokes about a Pope serving in the Devil's church. That would be too easy. However, it is a little poetic.

Regardless, the story of the church, as I was told it, goes something like this. They say the Devil saw the builder/architect fretting over the progress of the church. Supposedly, the builder was afraid he would not be finished before he died and he would never see his masterpiece completed. The Devil came and offered his services. Lucifer would speed up the process on the condition that no windows were within the church. I guess the Dark One liked the idea of the light not entering or something. Personally, I think the Devil should have been slightly more creative with his demands, but, a deal is a deal right?

Anyway, the guy agrees and the Dark Master gets to the speeding up part. With the church not finished, it was not consecrated ground, so, Satan was allowed to do his thing. However, when the Devil returned, it was consecrated. A good thing too, otherwise the Church might have been destroyed. The windows had been built and hidden by columns which stopped the Devil from initially seeing them from the foyer where he had made the initial agreement. When he worked out that he had been betrayed, he stomped his foot in anger, but did no more. There is the remnant of this footprint in the church today and if you stand in the same spot, it is true that many of the windows are obscured by the pillions. An interesting architectural design.

In addition, the legend says that when he came to inspect the church, he used the wind like a surfboard to get there. In his anger, he forgot to take his ride back home. So that is the traditional explanation for the perpetual winds in the church. Now, just a reminder, after this legend. This is where Pope Benedict worked. Curious choice. I'm sure it was just coincidence.

The rest of my time in Munich was spread between two

events. The first, was a visit to the Olympic arena and the nearby BMW showroom. Both were worth visiting. The BMW showroom was amazing. I got to sit in all these expensive cars and pretend I was a secret agent for a few seconds.

The second thing was the Stark Beer Festival. It is a festival for beers with high percentage alcohol content beer. Again, I didn't drink, but as this festival was in February, there were far fewer tourists and far more local participants. They really do wear those Lederhosen thingies.

You can make a lot of day trips from Munich. Unfortunately, I didn't have time or money or energy. Another one for the "next time list." After all the chaos in Munich, I headed north to continue my journey.

A very friendly stranger

Aside from Amsterdam (story coming up), I have only encountered prostitutes in one other location. Hamburg. I am told there is a Red Light District in Hamburg too and that females may not enter the area unless they are there to work. When I first arrived in Hamburg, it was snowing, cold as hell and I, as a typical Australian, was freezing and under-dressed. It was also night time and I was sick as hell. Still, there were places in the city to see and so I decided to do a little walk to orientate myself ready for the morning adventure.

I was moving slowly, because of the flu. My whole nose was blocked up with about twelve kilograms of snot and my eyes were like slits from the cold. That is a description of the more pleasant bodily functions I was subjected to at the time. While I won't describe the other symptoms for you here, I will say that they came from a different area of the body. Blockage was not the problem.

On my way back to the hostel, I unintentionally bumped into a lady on the pavement. It was nothing big, but I said sorry all the same. She smiled at me and said, in German, "Kein Problem." Thinking that was the end of our interaction,

I continued my walk. She followed and caught up. She started talking to me, first in German and when she realised my German was sub-par, she began to converse in English. She asked me where I was from, what I was doing in Hamburg, and what my plans were. I guessed she was lonely and didn't want to be rude, so I answered the questions as I continued on my way home. After I answered the above questions and was about to ask her about herself she simply turned and said, "Want to fuck?"

Of all the things in the world I was expecting her to say, it was not that. I looked horrible. I did not think that I looked at all in the condition for that sort of activity. I think that a team of Hollywood make-up artists would have struggled to make me look presentable. Flattered as I was (and not unrealistic about what was really going on), I politely declined. It was then that the second unexpected sentence came.

"Why not?" I now had to defend myself. The whole conversation had changed from a light chat to a debate on why I didn't want to have sex with her. So, I explained that, "It's not you, it's me. You are beautiful, however, I have a headache. So, perhaps in another life." I know, not my best lines (or anyone else's for that matter) but it was all that I could come up with. My guess is that she was cold outside and wanted to come inside. If she had asked for coffee, I probably would have been able to help with that. Either way, I felt terrible for rejecting her, surprised at the encounter and almost sorry that I couldn't invite her in. She seemed like a nice girl. I probably seemed like an idiot.

The rest of my time in Hamburg was quick. I only had half a day, did a tour, took a few snaps and moved on.

It was there the whole time?

Before I tell you this story, I must state a disclaimer. First of all, it was tough to get these next series of stories together chronologically. So, the rest of these Germany related stories

The Other Side Of Travelling

are a bit all over the place. Mostly in and around Berlin, they represent my adventures once I had moved to the city from my home town of Melbourne. The story of my big trip will pick up where I left off, on my way to Amsterdam.

A second disclaimer. This particular story you are about to read is about an army base called Vogelsang. I cannot recommend going to Vogelsang. In fact, my understanding is that, you are not allowed to go. So if you do end up going there, be aware you could potentially be in a lot of trouble. Also, be aware, it is quite dangerous. I read online that there was a landmine found in the area recently. It was a heavily militarised area and could hence have a myriad of potential risks. Don't risk it. Don't go and if you do, don't complain to me/sue me about it.

Now that the disclaimer is out of the way, let me tell you a little bit about Vogelsang. It is a former Soviet Army Base about an hour out from Berlin by train at a place called Vogelsang. The interest for me in going there was that, as far as I could gather from my research, it was largely abandoned and forgotten. It thus presented unique opportunities to see things as they were at the time.

The process to get there is not exactly easy. First, you have to take a train out of Berlin. The station itself is so small, that you must request that the train stop at the station. You do that by pressing a button as it comes close to the station and hoping that they remember to break. Once you get off the station, you have to head left. If you keep going, after a kilometre or two, you may see an old checkpoint gate. This is your clue. If you slide your bike under this and head directly to the forest you will find a road. Ride along this for about two kilometres and all of a sudden you arrive in another world. On your left, as you enter, you will see the remains of a mechanics workshop.

The word is that this base held nuclear weapons. My guess is that most of the soldiers and their families lived on base semi-permanently. As a result, there were quite some buildings that I would not have associated at first with a hardened

Soviet Army Base. For example, there was a supermarket and a theatre.

When I arrived, my first goal was to find the old statues I had seen online. All the pathways were overgrown with plants, but you could sort of follow where they were. It didn't take long before I was standing in front of a statue of Lenin, with the paint peeling off in the sun. There was something different about seeing it in this environment that gave it much more impact to me than if I had just checked it out at some museum. It belonged there, even if I didn't.

My friend and I explored each of the buildings. Eventually, we came up to a school. It was eerie. There were murals up on the wall of children. The paint was peeling and there were still many remnants that showed people had lived here. Parts of bikes and other pieces of material littered the area.

We went from room to room, sometimes requiring torches, starting on the top floor and making our way down. While much of it was very interesting, at the end of the day, the buildings were dangerous and falling apart. Sometimes trees were growing up through the floor. So, weirdly, it became a bit repetitive. "Destroyed room, destroyed room, ooohhhhh destroyed room with a tree, destroyed room." At the same time, it was too dangerous to let your guard down, so it was quite draining on the brain and body. I had a feeling about the school though and was sure that we would find something in the building that was worth the trouble.

After much-continued searching, I finally found the sort of thing I was looking for. Evidence of underground resistance. In a small room on the bottom floor, down a small flight of stairs situated just right of the centre of the building, completely in darkness, I slowly walked in and shone my light up on the wall.

It was there that I saw it. Some would say it is magnificent. Some would say it should be a World Heritage Site. I would use only one word to describe what I saw. Hasselhoff. Many Hasselhoff. Possibly all the Hasselhoff. Now that I think about it, what is the correct term for a group of Hasselhoffs? A pride of Hasselhoffs? A herd of Hasselhoffs? I would put my money on it being a swarm of Hasselhoffs. Everywhere I looked, the Hoff and his shiny 80s grin stared back at me. Someone had diligently taken the cuttings from Bravo magazine (a German kids/teens magazine) in great secrecy and pasted them all on the wall. The shrine of Hoff was their little rebellion. It was amazing.

In fact, if you think about it, it really captured a specific time. I can't imagine the Soviet Union being a fan of the Hoff and his song "Looking for Freedom". Musically, it was not my taste. It was also lyrically something that the Soviet Union was not always that interested in. If this person had put these photos up and been found out during Soviet times, they may have been erased from history or questioned about their musical taste. There was a specific time, when the Soviets still ruled, but the will of the people had dissolved the ability of the Union to tackle the influx of new ideas. Ultimately it led to its destruction. However, this was at a time, in between.

This homage to Hoff perfectly captures the mood during the time. There is no way of knowing when the posters went up, but the posters are from a late 80s edition of the magazine. They weren't printed from the net, they were clearly from the magazine itself. They must have been put up around the time of print or soon after. What an interesting find. For that alone, it was a worthwhile adventure. However, there was more to see. For example, with a little bit of inspiration and ingenuity, we were able to enter a bunker. It was dark, humid, and generally empty, however, there were Russian newspapers lying around which was interesting. Or I guess they would be if I could have read them.

Eventually, it got so hot outside that we made our way back. The mosquitoes swarmed around there, with all the dark, damp waterholes for them to multiply in. It was definitely an eye opener. For anyone interested, I went back to check in on the Hoff posters a few years later. As of April

2019, it is still there, untouched. What was new was a series of pieces of street art throughout the complex featuring a moody dog with various different interesting sayings. I was able to track down the artist. Their name is Tobo and the characters name is Erik. I put a few pictures at the end of the chapter for you to have a look.

Old, new and everything in between. This was one place that had a bit of everything. I was so glad I found it. I hope it is around for some time to come. Get off the beaten path occasionally. You never know what you will find.

You can trust me

By the time this story took place, I had been living in Berlin for about two months after the move. The weak European sun, though valiant in the attempt, was yet to destroy my mighty Australian tan. I was working at a school and there was an open day coming up. The school wanted me to impress the crowd. Normal stuff, happens at any school. I made a list of the things I needed for a whizzbang show to impress the kids and parents.

It was there that I hit my first snag. I had done a one month intensive German course and knew how to order fries at McDonald's in Deutsch. However, complex chemicals in German was sadly still beyond my limited language skills. So I tried to simplify where I could. For example, I managed to make acid base indicator out of cabbage juice. Easy enough and quite spectacular looking. Yet, I still needed one chemical that could not be found so easily. Hydrogen Peroxide. In normal percentages (around three percent) it is used in first aid kits. At around twelve percent, it is used to make the lovely bleached blonde N'sync look that was so popular in the late 90s. I wanted thirty percent. I wanted to break the bonds rapidly with a catalyst, so that it created a jet of coloured bubbly foam. A very impressive demonstration.

I asked my wife to go to a pharmacist and see if it was

The Other Side Of Travelling

possible to order it there. They knew her well and knew she was a nurse. They had no problem getting it for her, but said they would need a few hours to order it in. It breaks down relatively quickly, so they don't store it on-site. She explained that her husband would pick it up and they agreed.

So a few hours later, after work, I went to the pharmacist to get my chemicals. My wife looks very innocent. However, at this time, with my tanned skin, bearded face, crazy hair and very broken German it was a different story. She was hesitant to give it to me. The pharmacist wanted to dilute it down or get some extra confirmation. Eventually, I managed to convince her to give me what I needed after leaving a lot of details, such as ID, in case I came up on the nightly news as an attacker or something. It was a difficult ordeal, but I was glad to have got the chemicals I needed. It was going to be a good show.

I went to the next store on my list. I needed soil for a photosynthesis practical. I was going to run with the students later that week. I picked up my soil and headed off. I had the soil on my shoulder and had started walking back home. I had to pass the pharmacy on the way back. I saw the pharmacist in the window fixing a display. Without thinking, I did the normal Australian thing – I gave her a big smile and a wave. She looked mortified. I didn't understand. I assumed I had broken some German taboo by smiling at someone or something.

As soon as I got home, I explained the situation to my wife. As I was setting the scene with the way home, I was picturing myself from the perspective of the pharmacist. It was then I worked it all out.

The tanned skinned, bearded man with crazy hair, broken German and a bottle of a dangerous chemical that she had just sold, who called himself a "chemical teacher", now looked like he had a huge bag of fertiliser on his shoulder. For those of you more innocent readers, fertiliser is a known ingredient in certain home-made bombs.

I am surprised that I didn't have a SWAT team waiting for

me. I got the chemical to the school and did the show and wowed the kids with my "Elephant Toothpaste" experiment. It was cool, however, if I am honest, a little too much stress was involved for the result. The things one does for employment continue to amaze me.

From dream to reality

The best part of life is trying new things. Often when you are young, people assume you will try every experience offered, but as you get older, more and more people get stuck in their ways and fall into a rut. If you try to go against the grain of time, they look down at you. I am trying to fight that rut. So, at the age of twenty seven, with many years of air drumming under my belt, I found a pamphlet for a drum teacher. It seemed that he gave lessons nearby to my house and, so, I decided to just go for it.

Not that language is much of a barrier when it comes to music, however, as a relatively new resident of Berlin, with not nearly as much German under my belt as I should have had, I was worried that it would be a hindrance to the lessons. I sent a message to the number in broken German to explain that I would like lessons and that my German was not that good. The teacher wrote back that it would be possible and that the language would be no barrier to awesomeness.

I had sticks given to me by my wife, but nothing else and no real drum experience besides the aforementioned air drumming (it counts, right?). I arrived at the building. It looked like an old East German office building that had been converted for the purposes of practice rooms and it was very poorly soundproofed. You could hear the mix of many different styles of music blasting from different rooms, even from outside.

Arriving at the front door, I texted the teacher to announce my arrival and soon saw before me the drum master that would be taking me to the epic land of rock. He was an

The Other Side Of Travelling

interesting character. For a start, I couldn't work out his age. He had greyish hair which said that he was likely to be older than forty. The way he held himself however was so full with energy that pinpointing an accurate age was almost impossible. He wore chilled out clothing, mostly grey.

After a few flights of stairs, we entered the "office". It contained two chairs, smelt heavily of smoke and had a huge computer screen on the desk. There were drum parts everywhere. I was starting to doubt that I had the right place for me.

We discussed the business side of it and then we moved into the drum room. I stood down at one of the two kits in the room. Another kit sat opposite. However, he didn't go and sit at it. Instead, he stood in front of mine. He helped me to adjust the kit to my height and arm reach. Then the fun began. The lesson was already worth it before I played a note.

He started by explaining how to hold the sticks. I picked them up and even before I had the chance to ask, he was shaking his head. "You see these sticks? You hold them like this. Like a knife. It's a weapon." He showed me a grip and adjusted.

"Hit the drum" was his next instruction. I lifted my arm up to hit the snare. I asked, "Like this?" and was promptly stopped. "No No No." I looked up at him in confusion. I hadn't even done anything yet. The reasoning for the halt soon came. "Not like that. I see already what you are going to do. You don't hit the drum like that, hit it fucking hard. Let me see it." The next minute or so was simply me hitting the snare while he stood over me saying "Harder, Harder, HARDER." I felt more like I was about to enter boot camp rather than learn drums.

After he had established that I was able to hit the drums with sufficient force, he took to the kit. He started with explaining to me a few things and then we got started. I did OK. In fact, by my estimate, better than to be expected from a first lesson, which I wholly attribute to my air-drumming expertise. But, there was work to do.

After a few lessons, I started to get the basics. He was a really good teacher and was not nearly as intimidating as he appeared during those first moments at the kit. He always had a smile. At first it was always very professional, but after a while the guy started to loosen up a bit. I guess he was nervous with his English, but eventually got confident enough to throw a few jokes around. One day, we moved from standard grooves to offbeats.

My teacher seemed especially happy that day. He showed me the offbeat groove and explained the most common types of music it is used in. Yet, he still seemed to be holding back information. I could feel something bubbling inside of him. Finally it burst out.

"The best reason for the offbeat is to fuck up the fucking guitar player." I stared at him in confusion. He continued, "Imagine it now. The guitar player is playing a beautiful solo and then about halfway through, you change to an offbeat and SCREECH the fucking guitar player fucks the fucking thing up." The rivalry between the guitar and drums will continue for ages to come.

A simple matter of taking the initiative to learn something new, not only led to me learning a new skill, but also to meeting a nice dude and access to a world that I would not have otherwise experienced. So much fun. As a side note, the guy can really drum too. Maybe with another ten years of lessons, I might actually be able to jam with him.

The World is Going to End

Before we begin, a small intro for those of you that have never heard of Jello. He is the former singer of the 80s Californian punk band, the Dead Kennedys. Very outspoken, very political, very unique voice. He was bringing his new band (The Guantanamo School of Medicine) to the SO36 (the seminal punk club in Berlin) and I just had to go. I had another friend with me from Australia, Andy. My pal from Germany, Heinrich, came along too. I have already described Andy, but I should let you know about Heinrich. Heinrich had short brown hair. He had a well-trimmed beard on his face and wore glasses. He was studying hard to complete his university degree and happened to be one of the first people I met when I visited Berlin for the first time. I was lucky that we had stayed in contact ever since. Both Heinrich and I were massive punk fans, while Andy was going to be experiencing this world for the first time.

Heading to the SO36, we passed the club district of Berlin at Warschauer Straße. Interesting place, often with bands playing out the front. Not often my taste in music. This time was no different. Some electro band was playing. I guess people were digging it because there was a small crowd gathered and they were rocking, however, it was not for me.

To get the music out of our heads, we hurried even faster to the underground train station leading to the hip area of Berlin, called Kreuzberg. You will see all sorts of people there. We stopped off at a record store nearby to the venue and saw some cool stuff. Heinrich, Andy and I drooled over the limited edition pressings of some of our favourite bands. But we dragged ourselves away. Finally, a few minutes later, we arrived at the SO36.

There were two types of people there. New fans and the old-timers. The old-timers had their shirts on from the 80s with stains and holes in every place. A few had put on a bit of weight and had trouble fitting into them. But it was still cool. The new fans had a lot of Jello's t-shirts, including his most popular at the time "Nazi Trump Fuck Off" shirts. It was a good mix of people.

I knew it was going to be an interesting night because soon after I entered the venue, someone came up behind me. Placing his crotch against my butt, he began to thrust. I knew what was to be expected. I was supposed to turn around and tell him off for being so rude. The man would then proceed to crush my brain. I am not exactly a giant, don't know how to fight and am generally not fond of violence. I found myself in a tough position. I had to use other tactics. I chose my strongest weapon. Embarrassment.

As soon as I saw his friends watching and waiting for the reaction, I started thrusting back and winking at him. Now the man had a dilemma. He couldn't hit me for doing that, because he was doing the same. Even in the mind of this caveman there had to be some reason for the fight he was trying to instigate. Otherwise he would feel like the bad guy. Secondly, for him to pull out now meant that he had lost. The alpha male in him continued to struggle. So while I was smiling, winking and thrusting, he was thrusting back. His friends were laughing at him. Andy and Heinrich were looking very unsure of how to proceed. Alpha Man didn't know what to do. Confusion ran across his face. Eventually, he gave up and moved back to his friends who were laughing and pointing at him for some time. His face was quite red. I continued my conversation with my friends and waited for Jello.

Getting to the front of a concert hall is not too hard if you are lucky, and once again I managed to have both hands on the hallowed stage ready for the big man to come. Soon after, without too much bravado, the band came out and Jello, immediately took ownership of the stage. I know this because he accidentally stepped on my finger. I had Andy to my left, but Heinrich disappeared after about the third note. Andy was worried, however, knowing my buddy Heinrich, I assured my fellow Australian that we would see him soon enough.

They started with "Satan's Comb-Over". The second song was called "People With Too Much Time On Their Hands". I think it was new, but the chorus was easy enough that I was able to pick it up relatively quickly. Jello even bent down and we sang together for a while. Pretty cool, for me anyway. I am no singer and it may not have been so great for the audience to hear me over a PA. After a few more songs from his new band, one of the Dead Kennedy hits started. The floor went absolutely crazy.

About halfway through the song, I saw a familiar face behind me. Heinrich was back. He had no shirt, he was bleeding from a cut along the bridge of his nose and his glasses had been broken by a punch to his face. He had a massive smile on his face. My German friend was having the time of his life. Andy looked a little shocked. Heinrich and I simply nodded. We understood each other and words were not needed. Without one single utterance, but so much said, he melted back into the pit. Certain people live for this.

All in all, things were going well. The songs were grooving. There was a wonderful rendition of "Nazi Punks Fuck Off" which the crowd loved. I was really into it. All of a sudden, I felt an elbow in my back. Then a second, and a third. The elbow kept coming, searching for weaknesses. Finally, as it found my kidney, I couldn't ignore it anymore. I turned around to see a girl with hair dyed blood red, a black shirt and short skirt with fishnet stockings. She went to hit me again. She said, "I want to get through to the stage." I was not giving up my spot and said, "No." I asked her to stop it. After a few more elbows, I'm not proud to say, I pushed her back away from me. She fell down, but quickly got up and looked almost proud at me. She nodded and went off to find weaker targets.

It was coming up to the last songs, when all of a sudden, I saw the crazy lady on stage. She had managed to punch her way through someone, I guess. Jello had been playing "Holiday in Cambodia" and was on his knees with his shirt over his head for dramatic effect. He was mimicking being ready to be assassinated.

She grabbed his leg and started screaming at him, "Jello, I love you. I want your babies. The world is going to end. We have to fuck right now, on the stage. Take me Jello, take me!" Jello did not react. He was busy concentrating on the performance. So, the chick, leaving the love of her life, took a bottle of water and threw it around the stage before jumping back into the sweaty mess of a crowd.

It is important to remember that all these events happened while the shirt was over his face. He did not see the water hit the stage. He did not know it was there. Anyway, he pulled his shirt off, finished most of the rest of the song and decided to do a stage dive. He was right in front of me. I looked up at him. As I did, sweat dripped off of him onto my face. Pretty gross. I saw the look in his eyes. It was the look of a man calculating trajectories.

I could see in his eye exactly where he was aiming. He was going to go for it. His knees bent, and as I looked down, I noticed he was standing in the puddle made by his lost love. His knees began to rise as he moved to make the jump. I could see in my mind's eye what was going to happen, but could do nothing to prevent it. The knees straightened as he leaned forward over the crowd, face first. His shoes slipped. He fell.

Luckily he was mostly over the crowd already when the shoes lost their grip, so he landed and looked relatively impressive. However, unluckily for me, the way he landed resulted in his boot hitting me full in the face as he was pulled over. I got a nice bruise on my eyebrow for that one. Another great memory from the SO36.

After the concert was over, I managed to say a quick hello to the band and then moved over to the bar opposite. It is called the Franken and also plays very good music, very, very loud. If you get the opportunity, check out both. It is worth it.

We all came home, beaten, battered and smiling. I was sore for the next few days. Yet, every ache reminded me of the crazy night. May there be many more like that to come.

So, that is it for Germany. I now continue my narrative of my round the world trip. Off we go to Amsterdam.

(One lucky lion)

Daniel Greenwood

(Unverified, but perhaps a sinister sign lies underneath)

(My mighty cola in Munich)

The Other Side Of Travelling

(The Devil's footprint)

(Brandenburg Gate)

Daniel Greenwood

(Vogelsang, Lennon)

The Other Side Of Travelling

(Erik the wise dog, by Tobo)

(The Wall of Hoff)

Daniel Greenwood

(Russian Wall of Murals)

THE NETHERLANDS

If the price is right

I took a train from Germany to Amsterdam, shortly after my time in Munich and Hamburg. It is not often that I don't click with a city, but in the case of Amsterdam, it just was not for me. Just like Vienna before it, I just could not get the good vibes I was looking for there. Before we get to the bad, let's start with the good. The city is beautiful, especially with all the canals. Even when it is freezing, visually, it is a pretty nice place to wander through and get lost in. I visited the Anne Frank House, which was an eye-opener. Part of the eye-opener was the endless line to get into the place. Book online well before you plan to arrive in Amsterdam. You won't get in otherwise. It is a small museum, however, it has some impressive stuff to check out. The secret entrance to the hiding place was really well done.

There are memorials to those affected by the Second World War. What was unique, as far as I could see, was the specific memorial to the homosexuals affected by the Holocaust. There were interesting buildings, some compelling statues and, from what I am told, a number of cool pieces of art (which I couldn't afford to go and see). There are two things though, that make this city a little different from many others: Legal Marijuana and the Red Light District.

Firstly, a comment on the Red Light District. I did visit it a number of times, either to pass through it or to see and understand what it was all about. No, I don't mean trying the services available. I could barely look at the beautiful ladies in their windows. I figured that, I was not buying what they were selling, so I shouldn't be browsing. However, I was interested in watching all the other people, seeing who was checking the place out. What sort of people were drawn to a famous spot like that?

The variety was surprising. For example, the first time I went in, it was built into a walking tour (from the same company as the one run in Munich and Paris). So, various people from all walks of life entered as a group. We first went to the church near the main square. While we were looking at the church, the guide was explaining that the church was there to be ready to take the prostitutes' money to "absolve the sins" of the workers in the district. After some more history, he said, "Now, turn around."

Right there in a window, was a very, very curvy dark-skinned woman flaunting her wares. I looked behind me and forward. Church, Prostitute, Church, Prostitute, Prostitute, Church. It took me a good while to compute exactly what the arrangement was. What an introduction. Based on that, it seems that the rules of God were a bit more flexible around these parts.

A little further on the tour, it was explained to us that there were various sections, each tailored to specific desires. There is a main river that flows down the middle of the Red Light district. It is scenic. As I was looking out over the bridge, I was trying not to make eye contact with the two beautiful blonde girls to my left. They were tapping on the window and beckoning me to join them. As I drew my gaze away, I saw them. An old couple strolling through the district.

Of course, while initially surprised, I put myself in their shoes and quickly decided that I hoped to be that relaxed when I get to their age. I thought they both must be deaf. They were barely talking but making a lot of hand gestures. The female, in particular, was very active. She was pointing around at each of the windows as they passed. The man was looking down and shaking his head. I guess he was not so comfortable there.

But then, all of a sudden, the attitude changed. The woman pointed at a particular window about halfway between me and the next bridge. Instead of a shake, he gave a nod. She waved as he entered the room and continued off cheerfully down the river. I must say I was not expecting that. It definitely gave me a different picture of prostitution than what is presented in the media. I wonder if she went out and found her own too.

As a side note, if you leave the Red Light district on the side furthest from the main square, you will enter a world of amazement. Second-hand book-stores litter the side streets. If you like books and want to find something rare, you may have some luck there. There is even a book-store dedicated purely to second hand English books. Let me just say that I found stuff there that I thought would be impossible to get. I found a few books that were impossible to leave behind.

What sides would you like?

Anyway, we have dealt before with the Red Light District. There were many other instances of interesting human interactions, such as teenagers attempts to get into booths, but most of those are pretty predictable.

It is now time for us to turn to the part of the city that made my life in Amsterdam hell. The drugs. I can understand why people go there for it. It's legal and it's everywhere. The fast-food companies have a strong grip here, with fatty food going well with pot, I am told.

I did see a man with a KFC and McDonalds bag walk into Burger King. He walked out later and went to the fast food vending machines they have all throughout the city. From there he found a spot by the river and with a smile, as if he had just won a million dollars, and with tears almost flowing down his face, he opened each bag in turn and started to eat the food. Ships drifted slowly past in the canal behind him.

Tourists stopped and took photos of things around them. The guy just sat there, in his own world, continuing to enjoy his junk food.

After he had finished the food he had, he just stared at the empty bags. He looked lonely. In fact, he looked as if he had just seen the plane fly off with the love of his life and he knew that they would never come back. It was a look of understanding that it had to be this way, but he still wished that it could have been different. However, as it was food and not a lost love, he stood up, went to a Dunkin' Donut and soon found his groove again. That guy kept on trucking.

Who needs adventures when you have guests like these?

As for me, not being interested in drugs, after the walking tour, while most of the people were filing into the various coffee shops recommended by the guide, I went to the hostel for a small break. When I entered my room, there were not that many people there. Most of the people on the beds had obviously partaken in the use of the local delicacy, but were friendly enough. On the second night though, a new person arrived. Tall, slightly round in the belly, short black hair, glazed over eyes and a giant black hoodie. He was already rather odd to begin with, and his behaviour did not improve as the night went on. He must have taken something and whatever he took, it was not sitting well with him. He lay down on his bed, fully clothed with his hoodie over his head. He was staring at the roof. He kept saying, "I am the Devil." If he was, he wasn't a very good one. Yet, it did make the prospect of getting rest a little more difficult.

The next night, Devil Man was still around. He had, however, managed to leave the bed for a while. I guess even Satan needs food and to take a shit every once and a while. Yet somehow, the night ended up being worse than the one before.

I am a light sleeper in a hostel. I am all for the good vibes and fast friends thing, but at the end of the day, you are in

The Other Side Of Travelling

a room with a bunch of random people. Normally, on my travels, this has not been a problem. However, after Mr Lucifer did his thing, I figured that there might be some other drugs besides pot flying around this town. I was nervous and struggled to sleep easily that night.

As a result, it made sense that at around 4 am I was woken up by noises in the room. People arrive back to the hostel at all times of the night, so I figured they may have simply had a late flight in or a big night out. As my brain came into focus though, I began to count the beds and the people in them. It was an eight person dorm and there were already eight people there. Again, trying to reason, I thought perhaps someone had checked out already. Again, my fuzzy brain eventually found a problem with this logic. In the hostel, they still change sheets before the next guest arrives (or they tell you that they do anyway). No one came in to clean at this hour.

So, after running through a bunch of other implausible scenarios in my head, I came to the conclusion that the guy didn't belong here. But, he was pulling all his clothes off. He clearly thought that he was in the right place. He was looking around and soon enough, tried to get in bed with one of the girls in the bunk opposite mine. I had made friends with her over the past few days and was leaving Amsterdam that very morning. So I was told later by her, that at first she thought that I was just tapping her to say goodbye. However, I could see from my bed the colour drain from her face as she realised a naked man that she didn't know was trying to get into bed with her. She said no, but he kept trying. I got up and kicked him out. Admittedly, I didn't have to do much. As soon as I got out of bed, that was enough for him to realise that it was time to go. He made a lame excuse about thinking it was his bed and asked for his clothes back and then ran away.

The girl was rather upset, naturally, yet managed to calm herself down and notify the right people. I don't know what happened to that guy. I really hope he keeps himself to himself. That behaviour is uncool. As well as being generally upset with the situation, I was also upset with myself. I tried to break it all down for you here, but it all happened so quick. I still can't tell if he was just drunk and confused or more predatory. As far as my hostel experiences go, it was the worst. It is a timely reminder of the importance of being aware of the dangers of excess and the importance of consent. Be cool in hostels, so that everyone can enjoy their trip.

A mini tale

I didn't want to leave you with such a terrible story as the last encounter from Amsterdam. So, here is a quick one to lighten the mood. Back in Melbourne, a long, long time ago, I met a Dutch girl called Lisa. She had long blonde hair, was average height and was pretty good with photography. While I was in Holland, I managed to catch up with her. As well as spending some time in Amsterdam, she took me out to an old traditional town.

We did many things there,, but the one that I remember the most, was her forcing me to get into some clogs and ye olde clothing for an old school photo. She had said that she wanted to do it for ages, but, being Dutch, it was always a little awkward. Now that I was hear, she could use me as an excuse and just say that she was taking a traveller around to see the sights.

I was very sceptical at first, but, I'll admit here, that I had a lot of fun doing it. Don't tell her that though. This is just a little reminder, that, while we often try to avoid touristy activities, sometimes it is worth giving them a try. Even if it is just for a laugh.

Now that you have a picture of a hobbit in clogs, we can move on to the next town, Bruges.

The Other Side Of Travelling

(Holocaust Memorial for killed homosexuals)

(Red Light District)

253

Daniel Greenwood

(Interesting artwork near the church in the Red Light District)

BELGIUM

Are you sure this is safe?

By the time I left Amsterdam and headed to Bruges, I was sick. I mean, really, really sick. I was ten kilos lighter. It was making my movement a lot slower. I was sore everywhere. My nose was full of snot and the bowel movements were happening far too often for my liking. A seven-month trip is great, but when the choice is excitement or food, excitement often won, with dangerous consequences. However, there were still things to see and so, I pushed forward.

To be perfectly honest, the main reason I was in Bruges, was for the movie aptly titled "In Bruges". A great film with Colin Farrell. However, I wanted to see if Bruges was as boring as the film suggests it might be. If the mayor of Bruges was OK with the film, it has to be the most interesting marketing strategy for a city ever. Come visit us, we are boring. I hadn't thought that it would lead to an increase in tourists, but as I spoke to the people at the hostel, it drew more of a crowd than I could ever have predicted.

Upon first inspection of the city itself, it was beautiful, with lots of unique architecture and even some reasonably famous pieces of art. I took a boat tour around the canals and saw where parts of the film were shot. At the end of the second day though, I felt like I was close to being done with the city. It isn't that Bruges is boring, it is just that it is small. It does not take long to walk from side to side, up and down. Also, being sick, I was hesitant to move from my comfy warm seat for much, besides the awesome Fried Potato Museum.

Sitting in the hostel in the evening, checking my email, little did I know that things were about to change. I would not be having such a quiet night anymore. Out of the blue, two people came up to me. A guy and a girl, both around twenty years old. The lady's name was Elke and the gentleman's, Bryan. Both were blonde. Elke had a very stylish hairstyle and white earrings in. Bryan had really long hair that was tied back into a ponytail and a goatee. Neither were necessarily tall. They seemed nice and we got to talking. This often happens in the hostel and the themes are generally the same. "Where are you from?", "What are you doing here?" and "Where are you going next?" If your answers match with them, then you go into trading stories of the road.

However, I quickly worked out that they were, in fact, locals. Whenever you are travelling, locals are hard to get in contact with. So, I was not going to mess up an opportunity like this, as weird as the encounter was. We kept talking about various things. Eventually, Elke and Bryan must have decided that I was alright because the two invited me to a party. I thought, "Why not, what's the worst that can happen?" and I accepted their offer.

We left the hostel about twenty minutes after this. Normally, when I left the hostel, I turned right towards the city centre where I would navigate to the various attractions from there. This time, however, we headed left. After a short wander through the narrow streets, we ended up in the only colourful building in the entire neighbourhood, perhaps even in the entire city. Most of the buildings are not allowed to be altered due to Bruges' status as a world heritage city. Bruges is one of the most well-preserved medieval towns in Europe. The owner of this building had clearly not got the memo and had painted the exterior bright pink.

When we entered, the entire place was lit with candles. It was warm and cosy. I was glad to be out of the cold, given how poor a condition my body was in. The people there even offered me food. It was all nice, but I didn't see much of a party.

The Other Side Of Travelling

Most people were just chilling on milk crates or other makeshift furniture. Elke explained that, "The party is being held out the back of the first building." Bryan nodded reassuringly. I couldn't hear anything yet, but I followed.

Behind the building it was completely overgrown. I was basically climbing just to get through the grass. They obviously didn't have a gardener. There was even a slide which had been placed to get over some of the more unstable terrain. It was at this point that I realised, if the two wanted to kill me, they could do it and no one would ever hear about it. They probably wouldn't even know I was gone for a few days. It would take weeks for them to find my body, by which point, it would be a bloated disgusting mess. Maybe the cold would keep me decent enough for my family. My inner panic grew as I tried to keep an outer cool factor. We proceeded further into this jungle.

I was not alleviated of my panic as we began to enter what appeared to be a second abandoned building. I asked "What is this place?" Bryan told me cheerfully, "It's an abandoned monastery." This did not help to calm me down. I followed them semi-bravely forward. This building was lit with candles too. It was super eerie.

Elke said, "Let's go down to the basement." As we proceeded down the stairs, I could see that it looked more like a crypt. This was where they were going to murder me as part of their satanic ritual, I was sure of it. They'd lay me down, with a goat head and a pentagram, along with a few hooded figures. I just hoped it would be quick.

Finally, we opened the door and music came blasting through. There was experimental heavy rock playing. A band called "The Tragedy We Live In" was giving its all. There was beer and electric lights and it rocked. I watched their whole set, they played really well. After that, my blonde friends showed me the art gallery they had upstairs. Local artists had added graffiti to the walls. The art was abstract. While I can't say I understood it. However, it looked impressive and I was glad there was a place for these people to express themselves, in a town that was pretty, yet restrictive for alternative culture. It also seemed to me to give a place for people to practice their graffiti without defacing other buildings and getting into a lot of trouble with the police.

Finally, they introduced me to the "owner" of the Squat. He looked at me a little strange at first, but as soon as I mentioned I was from Australia, his whole attitude changed. He was ecstatic to have someone from so far away at his place. He told me to make myself feel at home, and if there was anything he could help me with, just let him know. Nice guy really.

Soon however, the word was out that an Australian was there. People wanted to meet me. Maybe they thought I had brought my pet kangaroo with me or something. A few were very kind and accommodating, offering me some of their speed. I politely declined, explaining that "I don't want to take that away from you, that it is a kind and generous offer. You should keep it for yourself." There was not much else I could do.

Eventually, I had to go. Not being well had caught up with me. I had started to feel rather dizzy. Yet, the internal fear of missing out on more of the amazing world that I had entered made me hesitant to leave. Still, I had further to travel over the next weeks and decided that if I destroyed myself today, I would miss out on many other things later. To be honest, it was too late. My body was already destroyed and I was running on fumes. However, I was still in a state of denial at that stage.

I said thanks to all the wonderful people I met. Elke and Bryan had shown me a side of Bruges that most people don't know exists. I'm glad I saw it. Maybe if you are lucky and keep an open mind, you will see it too. (Side note: As far as I know, the Squat has since been closed. Bummer right? But who knows, maybe your experience will be in another cool town).

This was almost my last stop on my "big trip". After Bruges, I went back to Berlin to visit friends and then flew to

Hong Kong. There, I was very sick and bedridden for two days. I managed to drag my arse out of bed and caught my uncle, who works in Hong Kong. I arrived back in Melbourne on Easter Day 2013. It was a great trip, but, as you can probably tell by the fact that this is not the end of the book, it was not the end of my travels. Going around the world was not enough. I wanted more.

Daniel Greenwood

(View of Bruges from the Belfry Tower)

(The Crypt)

The Other Side Of Travelling

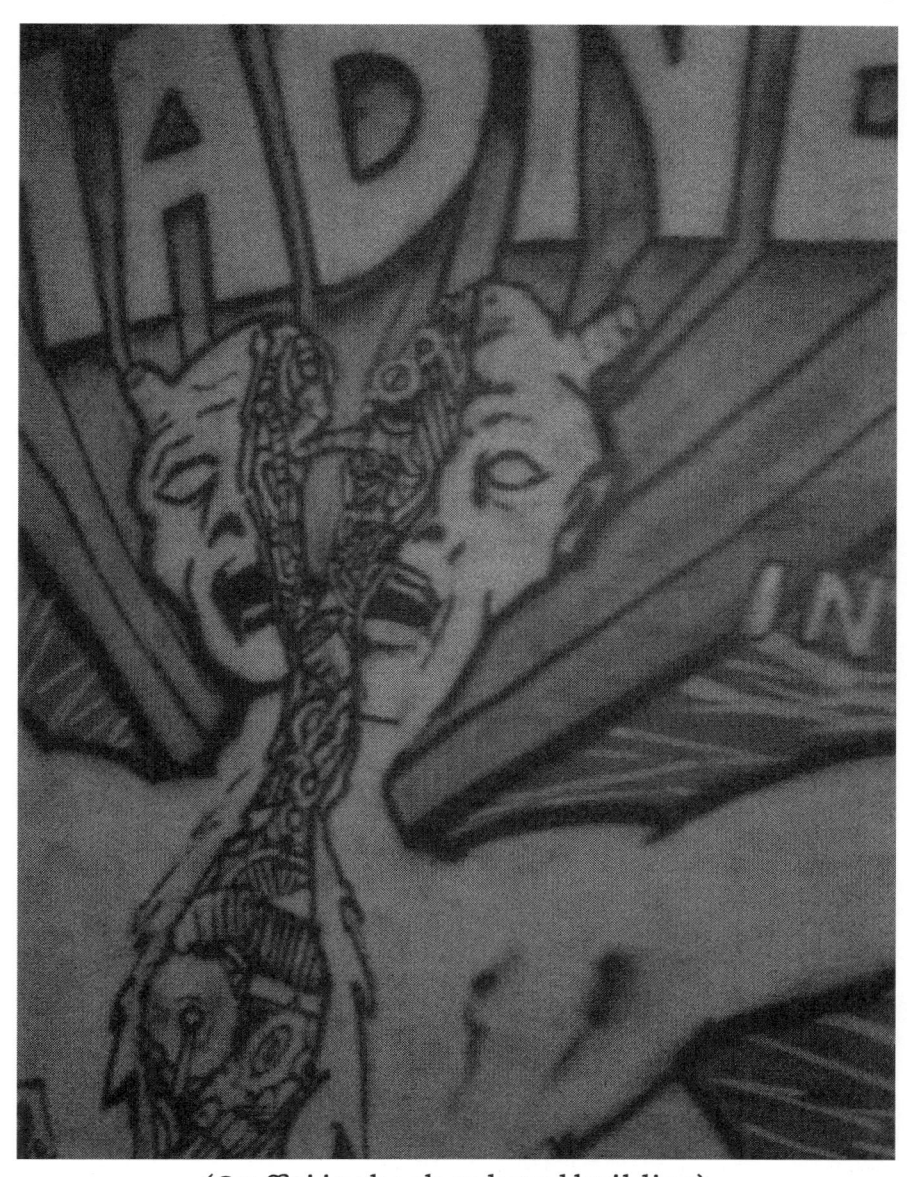

(Graffiti in the abandoned building)

TURKEY

The Walls Of Ruin

Seven months after my round the world trip, I returned to Europe. While over there, I took a detour and visited Turkey. I flew into Istanbul for five days from Berlin. I had a lot of preconceptions of how Istanbul was going to be and they were all immediately blown out of the water.

Istanbul is old, modern, and crazy. A wonderful city in all. McDonald's and KFC stand right next to ancient sites. Old and new are really intertwined here. After arriving in the old town and dropping off my bag at the hostel, I started by looking around the major sites. First stop was the Basilica Cistern. For any of you Dan Brown nuts out there, this cistern plays a big role in Inferno. It is an interesting place. You go down some steps and enter another world. They have lit everything up with a red tinge. I am not sure why. Maybe the red light does less damage to the structures within. The water level is quite low and you can see fishes swimming around. The famous head of Medusa is also situated there. There is a mystery about why the head is not upright. If I had to guess, I'd say that it has something to do with disarming the power of Medusa. However, I am no expert, so if someone finds the real reason, please let me know.

From there I moved to the Topkapı Palace. This is a sprawling palace in one corner of the old town. It has a lot of pretty gardens and old artefacts. Plus a lot of giant swords. You can go and look at the waterfront from the palace and see a lot of the newer sections of Istanbul across the river.

The Other Side Of Travelling

Finally, I looked around the Blue Mosque and Hagia Sofia. In the Blue Mosque, you had to take your shoes off, but the decorations inside were very detailed. The Hagia Sofia was where many of the Byzantine Emperors were crowned before the fall to the Ottomans. The new owners preserved the building, but "purified" it by removing a lot of the inner decorations that contradicted the new belief system. As you can see, from the short description, Istanbul has plenty to see.

All of these places are beautiful, yet full of tourists. Nice tourists, friendly tourists, but tourists nonetheless. I didn't want tourists. I do understand the hypocrisy of it all, being a tourist while hating other tourists, however, that is something I don't think about when I am in the country. As soon as I land, I can't help but think, locals cool, tourists annoying. The typical tourists move too slow for me, they are in the way, look more at their camera than at the object they are taking photos of, leave rubbish, disrespect the locals and get in my way. Did I mention that they get in my way? I hate when they get in my way. It is mostly the getting in the way that annoys me. I probably do as much damage in other ways. When I travel, I can only hope that I try to minimise my impact when I'm in my destination. Luckily for me, I am weird and what I want to see is often not something that is appealing to others. It is not often that I am there for something in the top five locations of a city.

What I desperately wanted to see was the Walls of Constantinople. They still exist from the ancient times, yet, are not exactly as well maintained as the more popular attractions. I don't understand why. I mean, think of the whole history of that city and that wall. This should be number one on the Istanbul list. However, as I said, I am weird, so my priorities are likely to be different to that of most others. Also, I think the walls must be pretty expensive to maintain. They are quite large structures.

So, the morning after my first day, I woke up and got the hostel receptionist to order a taxi. While I was waiting, I sat there in the semi-dark, listening to the first call of the morning prayer being blasted out of speakers from a minaret in the Blue Mosque. It was a blast of culture to my uncaffeinated body. I am not religious, but the call was quite relaxing for me and I was more than happy to sit and listen.

When the taxi driver arrived and saw that I was not from the area, he immediately wanted to take me to the palace. It was like he heard what I said, but assumed I had made a mistake. I had to stop him and I explained where I actually wanted to go. He looked at me very confused. He pointed at other things on the map, gave a thumbs up, then pointed at my goal and gave a thumbs down. After much sign language and a myriad of interesting facial expressions, I finally convinced him that I really, really wanted to visit the place. He shrugged. It was a small gesture, yet he seemed to be saying, "You give me the money, I'll take you there, but I think you are making a big mistake." I saw a similar expression once or twice from my mother when I was a kid and wanted to spend my pocket money on something she didn't like or understand. He turned on the fare meter and off we went.

When we arrived, he gave me another thumbs up with a face of confusion. I guess that he wanted to be very sure I was where I wanted to be. I looked outside and saw my target. With a huge grin I nodded, thanked him, paid him and walked towards the one part of the wall that was reasonably well maintained. The reason it was so well maintained was that it had been turned into an Ottoman prison, named Yedikule Fortress.

I arrived at the entrance and paid my five Turkish monies. Aside from the man at the gate, the place was absolutely empty. No security, no tourists. Just me and a set of ancient crumbling buildings. So, naturally, brimming with excitement, I began to explore.

It was really neat. You could climb up the towers and get a great view of the city, the water and the extent of the remaining part of the wall. I climbed up the staircase of one of the towers, only to realise how poorly maintained it was. An iron boardwalk wrapped around the inside of the towers leading to the top for views. I guess that it would have originally been a stone walkway, but it seemed to have crumbled away.

Halfway around one, I felt bending beneath my feet. At the height I was at, that was not a great feeling. Looking down slowly, afraid to make sudden movements, I could see the rusted iron. I am not sure if it was secure and I didn't want to wait to find out. On the other hand, I didn't want to miss the view, so I kept going. I was halfway across anyway when I made the discovery, it was just as quick to get to the top as it was to get back. I did eventually manage to get back to solid ground alive and I was probably overreacting. Even still, maybe they should change that out soon for something that looks a little more stable.

Eventually, after taking a photo of myself in front of the Golden Gate, which was incorporated into the fortress and originally the main entrance into Byzantine Constantinople, I left the prison and walked along the wall of Constantinople.

It seems that the wall is now used by the homeless people as shelter from the elements. Other sections were used for lovely garden beds. It is broken in parts and overall not in a good shape. Still, it had history and I was very glad to have been able to catch it. At the end of the day, the wall was still more sturdy after a couple of thousand years than some of the other buildings that the homeless people had available to them. So I guess, yay Romans?!?!?!

Grades and Negotiations

Once I had made my way along the majority of the wall's length, I arrived at a plaque commemorating the victorious Ottomans for taking over Constantinople. I had been walking on the side away from the old city. At this point, I crossed through the gate and entered back into the old world. I walked to the Grand Bazaar. On my way there, I even passed a few old aqueducts. I was so excited, I didn't quite know what to do or what to expect. Yet, I was aware you are supposed to barter or negotiate with the shop owner. When I entered though, I did not see the variety of goods that I had expected.

There was a leather section, a scarf and textile section, and a tourist section. It was not the chaos I had pictured in my head, although it was still interesting. So, after looking around, I decided on two scarves that I found at one of the vendors. One was an emerald green colour and the other a pale creamy white colour with some nice light blue woven through. They had beautiful patterns woven into them.

The shop owner introduced himself as Yunus. He was a nice gentleman, with rimless glasses, short hair and a jet black goatee and moustache combination. I showed him the two scarves I was interested in and he stated that, "I could have them both for the small price of a hundred and twenty Lira." At the current exchange rate that works out to be about twenty six Euros. This was something that I could not believe, it was already so cheap. However, my goal was to bargain, that was the experience I was after and therefore, I began the negotiations.

I am a terrible bargainer, but with a bit of forethought, one can negate this disadvantage. The trick I often use works something like this. Scope out the prices at a few of the stalls. From there, you should be able to work out how much you are willing to pay, and put exactly that much in the wallet. Then, remove all other cash and card and place it somewhere hidden. Now go to a new store that has the product you are looking for. Ask for the price and when they say it, try your best to negotiate. After a while, they will still probably be too high. So, your trump card is to pull out the money from your wallet and show them exactly how much cash you have. Simply explain that it is all you have and ask if they are willing to part with their goods for the full amount in the wallet.

If they say yes, you have yourself a bargain. If they say no, walk away, you can do no more. Also, don't be an idiot, when

The Other Side Of Travelling

you pull out your wallet, the only thing that should be in there is the money you are willing to part. If you have other stuff in there, pull the wallet out and get your ID stolen, don't blame me. More often than not, someone at a market will prefer the cash they can definitely get now, rather than the cash that they might get later.

By the end of our conversation, I had substantially reduced the price. I bought them, I looked happy and Yunus looked happy. That is, until I asked my next question. He was getting ready to say goodbye, but our adventure together had only just begun.

I started stage two of my adventure with a simple question. "So, how did I do?" Yunus looked confused with me. I repeated the question and then said, "Give me a grade." I wanted to know how well I had done in my bartering. Was I a black belt or just a green. A+ or an F? The shopkeeper still looked confused. Likely, he was trying to read me to see what I would say. If Yunus said I did terribly, maybe I would turn violent. If he said I did too good, perhaps I would not believe him. It was going to be tough to convince him to give me an answer. To get him to give me an honest response would be even more difficult.

After much assurances that no matter what score I got, I would be happy, he finally told me. B+. Yunus began to explain that, "If you had come a little earlier, maybe you could have got a slightly better deal." He also said that I had maybe not started at the right number for the negotiations. Yunus nervously waited for the punch with a scrunched up face. It obviously didn't come and when he looked at me through slitted eyes he saw my huge grin. We hung out for a while afterwards and had some tea. It was a nice chance to chat and learn something about the place I was hanging out in. He seemed to enjoy the distraction. When another potential customer came along, I let him be. He had work to do. Overall, it was a good day.

Daniel Greenwood

Schliemann Strikes Again

The next day I took a two-day tour to Troy and Gallipoli. It is quite a way away from Istanbul, however, the entrance to the Dardanelles has always been important for many civilisations. I mean, doesn't the name Troy say enough? If the battle did occur, I doubt it was all over a woman. More likely, it was for control of this highly strategic location.

I would be based in Ecebat. From there, my tour guide would pick me up each day and take me to the important locations. My tour guide for Troy was an interesting man. For reasons I can only guess at, he was obsessed with Australian sayings.

As soon as he found out I was from the "Land Down Under" he was throwing slang at me like there was no tomorrow. "Would you like some dead horse?" or "I can give you a stick in the eye for lunch." He asked me if I had any other ones. I went through the exhaustive list that I had learned throughout my years (mostly from my Aunty and Grandpa), but he knew almost all of them.

He started spewing them out so fast and hard that I didn't follow or understand half of them. At the end, I wanted to give him my Australian passport. He was more Australian than I was. I guess it makes sense too. This is a big area for Australian tourists. He must have had a lot of them come through and teach him everything they knew. Either way, he was the master and I was the apprentice in that exchange.

We took a van from the hotel and drove onto a car ferry, which took us across to the other side of the Dardanelles. From there, there was a short drive and we arrived at our destination. Troy was pretty poorly preserved, mainly because our main man Schliemann the demolition man decided that Priam's gold was somewhere around here (you may remember his name from the Tholos tombs in Mycenae).

He didn't bother to check that there was up to seven layers

The Other Side Of Travelling

of archaeological infrastructure above his desired location, he just dug straight down. There is still today a trench left bearing his name. I guess he would be proud, but most archaeologists look at it in dismay and disgust. You can still see fragments of destroyed temples from his "work" on the ground. I have a feeling all the Greeks in their hunt for Helen did less damage than this guy ever did. If you ever get the chance, you should look up more on this guy. His life is an interesting story to read about.

We found where they think would have been the "Palace of Priam" and on our way out climbed up a giant wooden horse like we were Achilles waiting to let loose. It was cheesy, but given the legend of Troy, you couldn't really expect anything less. On the way back to the boat, we saw the wooden horse used in the Brad Pitt film "Troy". It had been donated to the city after filming was done. It looked pretty cool, too.

In the evening, we returned to our base in Ecebat. At first glance, it would seem to me that the city is doing well. However, very quickly, a walk behind the first row of streets showed abandoned buildings. That's when I began to see how hard places like this were hit by the financial crisis. They had a facade which they maintained at the hotel district, but beyond that there was not much going on. I wonder what would happen if Australians stopped going there. Would the town exist? Tourism as an economic model can be both beneficial and a huge drawback for cities. Interest in locations can dry up quickly as trends in the "coolest" places to travel change rapidly. I hope the town survives, the people there were really friendly, to me anyway.

Off the beaten path

The next day we moved on to Gallipoli. This time, it was on the same side of the river as Ecebat, so we didn't need to take the ferry. We started very, very early, with the first stop being a Turkish memorial, overlooking the sea. Throughout the day, we visited actual battle locations and memorials for all the major parties in the conflict. It was a humbling experience for me.

Australians are taught about the story of Gallipoli as though it is a heroic act. While the Turkish are friendly, they don't quite agree on how things went down and the sequence of events. At the end of the day, the story sort of ends the same, but the details in between were reasonably different. Seeing the locations was thought-provoking and gave me goosebumps. Once again, seeing the trenches still there, I got the distinct feeling of not wanting to ever be a part of something like that.

As part of the tour, we were taken to a new museum that had been opened to tell the story of Gallipoli. I think they had it ready so it could be there for the centenary of the battle. The tour guide was very proud of it. It was some sort of 4D theatre museum. They were polite about the Australians, however, as I said, the fine details were slightly different to those that I grew up with. It was an interesting experience and made me question which side of the story was true, or perhaps, they were both true? Travelling is good for making you question your values and built-in understanding to perhaps come to a more realist view of the world.

After this, we visited a number of the grave sites where various soldiers had been laid to rest. I was looking around and seeing what I could. I noticed a small path leading off to the left when I was facing the beach. Looking around and not seeing anyone interested in a small hairy hobbit like Australian and his adventures, I ran down the path to see what I could see.

There on the beach was some kind of concrete defence. It must have been from WWI or WWII, based on the style of its construction. It is very likely that it was originally higher up on the dunes. However, it appeared that it had now slid down with the erosion of the dunes and was sitting at a funny angle on the beach front. There was a sheer drop of about four metres high from where I was to the beach. Not high for most people, but for a short man like me, it was enough to second guess whether going down was a good idea. I looked around and, as far as I could see, I was still alone. So seeing that there was a few grip holds that would hopefully let me climb back up to meet the group, I slid down the face of the hill and explored the structure.

The structure itself was about two meters high and just under two meters across. There was not much within aside from rubbish and it was very dark inside. Only small slits on three sides, which I guessed were for the use of a gun, and a rusted doorway let any light in. I thought it was fascinating and was just trying to take a moment to reflect on nature taking back what man left behind, when I heard voices.

I looked up, to find that half of the tour group was watching me. They were staring at me as if I had done something sacrilegious. I waved at them and beckoned for them to come and have a look. They all shook their heads. I shrugged and continued my observations. They continued to observe me. It became very awkward. I didn't think I was that interesting. Eventually, it was time to move on. I started the climb back up to the path. The others just watched me, with grim faces. It was slow progress with the sand sliding out from under me. I eventually got up. No one helped me, they just looked at me and "tutted". I tried to break the ice and asked them if they knew what the next stop was. They just shook their heads and walked off.

To this day, I don't quite know what I did that was wrong. If I had to guess, I was travelling with people who were used to travelling on tours and the thought of breaking away to check something else, not on the schedule, was heretical. I also guess perhaps they were confused as to why I would spend my time looking at that structure, rather than at the names of the soldiers buried in the field. Either way, the reception was frosty when I got back on the bus.

After going to a few more trenches and soaking in the landscape, I returned to Istanbul. The way back involved a long, awkward bus ride. When I got back, I spent a few more days enjoying myself and exploring the city.

Super Economy

Early, on my last day in Istanbul, I had booked an airport shuttle to pick me up from my hostel. I was going to fly from there to Rome to meet my partner. I was waiting outside, listening to the morning call to prayer, when the shuttle arrived.

I had a look in and could clearly see that there were no spare seats for me. I hoped that someone was staying at the hostel and would come out of the bus, but no one did. The driver came out to greet me. He took my bag, put it in the back of the van and then guided me into the vehicle. I figured he would be empty-handed. However, he had something special, just for me, that he had brought with him from the back. I took one look, understood what it was, and realised that I was in for a memorable ride.

Smiling, he put a small, yellow, plastic step/stool on the floor of the bus. He told me that I could sit there. There would be no safety belt. The seat was not attached in any way. I would be facing everyone else and hoping that I didn't make a big mess in my pants as he turned corners. I had no other choice, I had to get to the airport and I didn't feel up for arguments. I had paid for a seat on the airport shuttle and one had been provided for me. What more could I ask for?

Getting on the bus and greeting those around me, I had the smoothest ride to an airport I have ever had. However, no matter how well the guy drove, my knuckles were white as I held on for dear life. The sheer thought of a crash or some other unfortunate event made my heart beat almost out of my chest. Finally, the trip ended. We had arrived at the airport. It was cheap, quick and efficient. I am glad, but I'm not sure I would take that particular method again.

As I looked out the window of the plane, I thought more

about my time in Istanbul. It is a great city and a great country with lots to see. I hope one day, I can go back. I'm curious as to how Yunus is doing.

Daniel Greenwood

(The WWI structure)

(Schliemann's Trench, Troy)

The Other Side Of Travelling

(Left over trenches from WWI, Gallipoli)

(Yedikule Fortress Tower)

275

Daniel Greenwood

(Yedikule Fortress)

(Wall of Ancient Constantinople)

The Other Side Of Travelling

(Grand Bazaar, Istanbul)

(Blue Mosque)

HUNGARY

A series of random adventures

In 2016, I flew to Budapest with Andy (the guy who had joined me for that Jello Biafra concert). When we landed, we got an immediate feel for the attitude of the city. I had bought a bus ticket and as the bus arrived, the doors opened, some people went in. When it was my turn, I stepped in and the driver closed the door on me. I was in, but Andy wasn't. More importantly, my bag wasn't either (sorry Andy. Priorities). The door was literally closed on me and I was stuck. The bus driver didn't open it. He just screamed at me and yelled in Hungarian. I didn't understand a word. Finally, after a good minute (it felt like ten), he opened up the door, I stepped backwards and then he shut it on me. Still glaring, he sped off as fast as the old bus would allow. Not the welcome I had hoped for.

Eventually, Andy and I were able to catch the next bus, got some cash out at a local shopping mall and then for the rest of the way, took the train from the bus station. We found our hostel, which was down a crazy back alley, yet, relatively near the Parliament, which was great. The first day, we simply grabbed a map and started walking. It was August though, and extremely hot. We saw many things, trying to keep close to the main river flowing through the city.

Our first major destination was to walk up a hill, to get a good view of the river, with its many bridges spanning the gap and the city itself. While up on the hill, it was easy enough to walk to the castle, through the castle and down the hill, past a bridge with a bunch of lion sculptures. The final stop

The Other Side Of Travelling

on the way back to the hostel was a Holocaust Memorial in front of the parliament building. Very well done and very well photographed. With the sunset in the background, around forty tourists tried to take photos including the memorial, the river and the sunset. We tried to get ours too. I think mine turned out alright in the end.

Andy was in architectural heaven. He loved the designs of the buildings and the sculptures. I liked it too and found it less touristic than Prague had been and was happy to hopefully get closer to a real picture of the city. I hate to admit it though, the heat and humidity were killing me a little. I normally prefer to travel in winter and this was about as far from winter weather as it gets here in Europe.

The next day, we went to the market. My goal was to buy some paprika powder. I am a big fan of spicy food and I had heard that this famous spice from Hungary was the best. The market was really cool, but I didn't understand exactly how it worked.

At one of the stalls, I saw a bunch of stock out the front and a few more items behind what appeared to be a counter. However, there was always a small gap in the wall that I assumed was the entry. I tried to walk in, but was stopped quickly. The lady was super angry with me. She explained it was the storage for the store. The only thing for me as a customer was everything out the front. I was pretty embarrassed and in hindsight it made sense. However, in the first place, it really did look like an entrance for shoppers. I bought a large bag of paprika and picked up a puzzle box from upstairs that looked good. There was not much in the way of bartering there which was a surprise for me. Andy picked up his presents for the family. After another quick look, we continued on our way.

This time, instead of heading towards the river, we made our way more towards the city centre. We found a great series of second-hand book-stores. Many had a small selection of English books. However, what was interesting was to see the number of academic books there. There were books by authors I would never dream of being able to pick up in a normal second-hand store in England or Australia. This showed to me the appreciation the Hungarians had for culture and study.

Like the video game?

After we had spent a few more days wandering through the city, checking out the parks, museums and other sights, we decided that we would go to a gun range and try a few communist-era weapons. For Andy, it was a chance to see how the guns were different from those he had used in the army. For me, it would be my first time shooting. I can't say I was excited, but I was hoping that I would gain an understanding of the gun culture if I gave it a shot. I will never stop making puns. I can't help it.

We took a taxi out to the shooting range. I have a feeling that it used as a strip club in the evenings. I came to this conclusion based purely on its cheesy décor. But, for our activity that day, we were led into a different room. A giant, hairy hulk of a man was waiting for us there and handed us the weapons. He was also making sure that we didn't do anything stupid. We started with a pistol and worked our way up to an AK-47. There was a short explanation before each weapon was handed to us and the employee stayed very close while we had the weapons in our hand. After all that, we then went to another room where we tried out a shotgun. I did OK with most of the weapons, but got a big bruise from the shotgun, as I didn't lock it into my shoulder properly. I did hit all the targets though. I wonder if that means I was good or if they had simply put the targets so close that you couldn't possibly miss. To finish off the experience, after we were done with the guns, the guy gave us each a beer. I gave mine to Andy.

I have to say, after having done that, I still can't understand the hype about guns. I didn't get a rush, I just felt like I was cheating. Point and click. Sure, with training, you can be more accurate, but at close quarters, simply point and shoot. Not

The Other Side Of Travelling

for me. Seems too cheap a way to sort out one's problems.

Sneaky Sneaky

One of the most difficult days in Budapest was when we tried to find and enter an abandoned train yard. I like to find the more abstract locations in any given town. I had read somewhere that there was supposedly a communist-era train with carts from WWII left over. This was something I had to try and see.

Andy and I took a train out from the main station of Budapest early in the morning. Once we arrived at the station, we followed the instructions I had found on the internet. We took some side roads and then crossed the tracks, until we found a path heading behind the station and towards a back entrance to the train-yard.

The yard was still being used for modern trains. Yet, there was a significant section with dilapidated train parts and other interesting bits and pieces. We snuck in through the back entrance and kept the broken train parts to our left, to try and use as cover from the workers setting up trains. We kept moving as far as we could, admiring the broken down trains and carriages when possible. We hopped into a few carriages and looked around. Others had been there before us and filled sections of the abandoned trains with graffiti. Some pieces were OK. Most were not.

Eventually, we hit a snag. The fabled train was over in a shed directly in front of us, across a field. The problem was, about halfway there, our cover disappeared entirely and there was nothing but open field between us and the shed. On top of this, there was a watchtower to our right, so we would be exposed on both fronts. We couldn't see if anyone was in the watchtower due to the sun glare on the glass. It was impossible to make a judgement. It was too far to simply just run. Maybe Andy could have made it, but as we have previously established, I am not fit. I travel light because it is the smart thing to do and also because I am extremely lazy.

We sat there for a good twenty minutes, looking for signs or another way into the shed. We couldn't go along the fence to our right, it was just a wire fence and would give no cover. The grass was not long enough to crawl. The entrance to the shed itself looked like it was pretty close to a building in use by the workers. From what we could see, the door was closed. We would be taking a risk and it could still be that the place was locked up.

It was no good. I am embarrassed to say, that we eventually chickened out. There was no clear way across and the chance of being in trouble with the police in Hungary was not something I wanted to have to deal with. Alas, we made our way back. To this day, I'm still bummed out that we didn't make it. Maybe next time I will have the guts.

Once again, a disclaimer. I don't recommend attempting this. The risk of getting caught and getting in a lot of trouble is high. So, don't be stupid, try one of the really cool things that won't get you in the bad books of the police.

When Andy and I got back to the hostel, as we were unlocking the door to our room, a guy appeared out of the roof to our left. Yes, you read it right. The roof. We were a little shocked to say the least. Tall and bulky, with flaming red hair, he said "G'day."

We worked out that he had come out of the roof above us using a small ladder to our left. He seemed to come from Australia. I asked him, "Are you staying here too?" I was curious if there were more rooms up the ladder. The red-headed man answered both questions with one answer. He explained that he was the watchman. The small room above was a sleeping place while he was on duty. He further explained that, "This is a good job for me. I can have a place to sleep, don't have to pay rent, get a bit of cash and don't violate my parole." This last part piqued our interest.

I asked him, "What do you mean?" The guy pulled up his pant leg to show a tracking anklet. He seemed a little proud of it, though didn't tell us what it was for. It didn't necessarily build confidence in me leaving my valuables behind.

What a...um...generous gift

Following the failure at the train yard, I wanted to find something amazing to make up for it. After a bit of research, I managed to find an old Roman fort, which we checked out. However, after a few days of intense walking in the summer heat, my friend, just out of the army, was done. He wanted a break. He joked, "I did enough walking for the last four years. I want a holiday man, not another expedition." He would take a rest at the hostel. However, I wanted to keep going. I had a free ticket to a museum.

So, I left my friend behind and went back out to the hot sun to see the museum in the castle. It was pretty well done and the basement had some of the foundations showing how it might have looked back in the days, when it was first built, which was interesting.

After I was done, I was walking around the outskirts of the castle. It was nice. There were lots of trees and lush grass. It was not necessarily shady, but with the trees it just felt a little cooler. Any advantage in that heat was welcome. In the park, a couple was having their wedding photos taken. They looked like a really handsome pair. The guy was a tall, muscle-bound giant of a man. The lady was a very good looking, skinny lady with light brown hair and a very expensive-looking dress. I looked in my wallet. I knew how expensive weddings could be, having paid for one myself rather recently. I was leaving Budapest the next day and would be unlikely to use the Forints that I had in my wallet before I went. So I gave the couple a thousand Forints and tried to walk away saying good luck.

They wouldn't let me go. More specifically, the groom wouldn't let me go. The bride looked pissed off that some sweaty hairy guy was interrupting her photo shoot. But the groom insisted that I get in there and take a photo with the couple. After a little discussion, I did it quickly and tried to get away. They wanted my email to send the photo to me. Sadly, the photo never came.

    I walked away feeling good about myself and headed back to the hostel via the Chain Bridge and the Parliament building. I continued to feel good, right up to the point when I saw a money exchange store near the main train station. As I sat there, looking at the exchange rates, I felt embarrassed. I kicked myself. I cursed my own stupidity and ignorance. A thousand Forints, at the current exchange rate, equates to about four euros. I had interrupted them to give them the equivalent of tips for a cup of Starbucks coffee. No wonder the bride was pissed.

    I generally recommend doing nice things for people, or as the people on the internet say, random acts of kindness. However, just make sure it actually is a "random act of kindness" and not just annoying. I failed that rule for this one.

The Other Side Of Travelling

(Cityscape, Budapest)

(Bazaar, Budapest)

Daniel Greenwood

(My target at the shooting range)

(Abandoned Train Yard, Budapest)

The Other Side Of Travelling

(Abandoned Train Yard, Budapest)

(Roman Arena, Budapest)

Daniel Greenwood

(Couple were having photos taken right around the corner at the Budapest Castle)

FINAL THOUGHTS

Over the course of this book, I have given you some of my more memorable stories that I lived through on my travels. At the time, many of these stories were about annoying, frustrating moments. Later, as I look back, they became some of my favourite experiences. I definitely did not always keep my cool, but often, people came out of nowhere to help me and save me from a terrible time.

Despite what governments and various reports say, more often than not, people all over the world just want to help. Sometimes the smallest gestures ended up helping me the most. So, firstly, thank you to all those who have helped me on my travels. Often, I think about all the hard work I put into making those trips happen, but really, I would not have gotten half as far as I did without the help of all those people that aided me throughout my travels.

Secondly, if you get the opportunity to help and you can, do it. I am not talking about giving your life savings away or anything, but sometimes you could see someone that needs a coffee or something. Little acts have big impacts. You never know when you might be in that position one day.

I hope you found this book entertaining and that you were inspired to write a few of the names down on your travel list for a future holiday goal. Until next time, keep on travelling.

ABOUT THE AUTHOR

Daniel is a small, hairy hobbit like creature that has an unhealthy obsession with history and travel. Born in Australia, he now lives in Berlin. He also has the problem that, once an idea is in his head, he can't rest until it is finished. Two years ago, without any writing experience, he started to write a book. He could only draw from the world around him and decided that the people out there are far more interesting than any fancy fantasy world he could come up with. So, he wrote down his tales.

Now, he has two books under his belt. The first, "Where Next?" is what he loosely calls a "travel guide". Really, it is just a list of places that he drools over whenever he thinks of returning to a location. You will have to work out transport and all that stuff for yourself, but if you pick up "Where Next?" at least you will know where the cool places are. Or, more specifically, the places that Daniel thinks are cool.

Obviously, the second book is "The Other Side of Travelling". These are the stories that keep Daniel on the road, looking for more adventure. It wasn't always glamorous, but the people he met along the way really reminded him of all the wonderfulness that exists in the world.

He runs a website, with articles that you can check out to keep you busy. He also has a podcast series, if you are into that sort of thing. Daniel was never the "creative creature", so he named the podcast series "The Other Side of Travelling".

The Other Side Of Travelling

Daniel tells me there is a lot more things to come. Some travel related, some not, but keep an eye out. December 2019, he hopes to put out the sequel to "Where Next?", but, well, he is a perfectionist, so don't hold him to it.

Daniel also told me to say thank you for taking the time to look at this book. He really appreciates it.

Daniel Greenwood

Where Next?

A mini travel guide to 20 of your favourite destinations around the world.

Available Now!
Get more information on the website:
www.dgreenwoodbooks.com

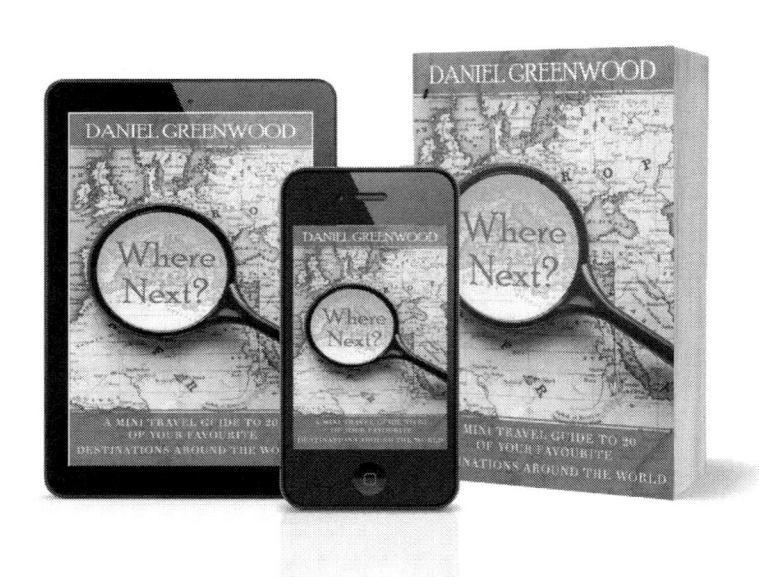

CREDITS FOR IMAGES USED IN BOOK COVER

Front Cover: iStock artist © pcruciatti Stock photo ID:472010429

Back Cover: ID 66682183 © Ekaterinabelova Dreamstime.com

Made in the USA
Middletown, DE
10 May 2019